Martha! Martha!

The Third Spiritual Adventure

Martha M. Brown
Freddie M. Lindsay-Payne

*Priority*ONE
publications
Detroit, MI USA

Martha! Martha! The Third Spiritual Adventure
Copyright © 2013 Martha M. Brown & Freddie M. Lindsay-Payne

Unless otherwise notated, all poetry submissions herein are © Martha M. Brown.

Due diligence has been made to determine the origin of all entries marked *Anonymous*. Should authors of these entries become known appropriate permissions and citations will be noted in subsequent printings of this book.

All rights reserved. No part of this publication may be reproduced, stored in a retrieval system, or transmitted in any form or by any means – electronic, mechanical, photocopy, recording, or any other – except for brief quotations in printed reviews, without the prior permission of the publisher.

*Priority*ONE Publications
(800) 596-4490 Nationwide Toll Free
P. O. Box 34722
Detroit, MI 48234
E-mail: info@p1pubs.com
URL: http://www.p1pubs.com

ISBN 13:   978-1-933972-33-6
ISBN 10:   1-933972-33-5

*Editing, cover, and interior design by Priority*ONE *Publications*

Printed in the United States of America

CONTENTS

Preface 7
Motivators and Inspirators 9
About the Author 15
About the Co-Author..17
GENERAL THEMES 19
    Is the Bible Really True? 21
    Reality Checks of Biblical Origin...23
    The Gift of Love 25
    Renewing Our Commitment to the Christian Doctrine....................26
    The Inner Conflict 30
    The Two Controlling Spirits...34
    The Comes of Discipleship 36
    The Need for Increased Laborers in the Vineyard 38
    Four Types of Workers 40
    Christian Stewardship 42
    Challenge to Choose Wisely 44
    We Are God's Building...46
    A Spiritual Awakening 49
    The Resurrection 51
    Christian Rejoicing in Commitment..53
    Recognizing the Fruit of Committed Lives 56
    The Woman Who Brought Others to Jesus 61
    Living in a Warring Society 64
    The Peaceful Role of Women in Society 66
    Young People's Role in Society 69
    Christian Parents Commended 70
    My Christian Mother..73
    The Basic Four R's of Reaching Teens 74
    Using Time Wisely...77
    God's Miraculous Saving Power in 1987 80
    My Hero...81

Have You Lost Someone? 82
　　Have You Lost A Bible? 83
　　The Body of Christ 84
　　The Hand of God 86
　　Patience 88
　　Longsuffering 90
　　Clothings 92
　　Christian Dress Code 93
　　Autumn 94

HISTORIES 96
　　History of Father's Day 97
　　History of Mother's Day 98
　　The History of Children's Day 99
　　Easter 100
　　Thanksgiving: A Harvest Festival 101
　　History of Woman's Day 103
　　Contributions: People of Color in Bible History 105
　　History of the Women's Army Corps 108

TRIBUTES & DEDICATIONS 113
　　Ode to Martha 115
　　Tribute to Mrs. Martha Ishmael-Brown 116
　　Our Dear Aunt Martha 118

SPECIAL SUBJECTS / WOMEN'S MINISTRIES 120
　　Living from the Inside Out 121
　　Women Finding Favor with God 124
　　Walking in Your Season 127
　　Sista Girlfriend 130

POETRY 131
　　Now is the Time 133
　　Spiritual Growth 134
　　If Jesus Would Come to Your House 135
　　Go Ye 136
　　I Love You Lord! Why? 137

    Footprints on Purpose 138
    Morning Gratitudes 139
    On Being Accepted by Others 140
    What Shall I Render? 141
    Open Mine Eyes..142
    Morning Thankfulness 143
    The Desirable Gift 144
    Whom Shall I Send? 146
    Meeting the Standard..147
    Appreciation 148
    Fragility of Man...149
    Distressed Moment 150
    Youth's Wait..151
    Mother's Influence 152
    An Evening Prayer 153
    The Ever-Present Lord 154
    Beatitudes of the Aged 155
    Hypocritical Singing..156
    Pensive Mood 157
    Thy Will Be Done!..158
    Crossing Over..159
    True Friendship...160
    God's Little Squirrels 162
    Is Anybody Happier…?...163

DRAMATICS 165
    In the Beginning...167
    The Ten Commandments – Part I & Part II..170
    Racing with Father Time – Part I & Part II 177
    Return of the Wayward Son..184
    Deliverances (Easter)...186
    Gratitude Unlimited..188
    We Three Kings of Orient Are 190
    Christmas: Decorative & Spiritual 193
    Resources 199
In Loving Memory of Mr. Granderson Brown 200
Memorial Meditations..201

PREFACE

This dedication is to the Ishmael Family, Pastor Bernard Smith and the Warren Avenue Missionary Baptist Church family in Detroit, Michigan.

"To God be The Glory for the Great Things He has Done"

The zeal for this third sequence of "Spiritual Adventures" was not mine, but the Lord's. He placed it in the mind and on the hearts of Bernyce and Margie my nieces, who were pleased to be on board. Thanks much.

As you travel this highway to your destination, you will find enhancing Biblical Truths for your children and their generation.

Our fervent prayer is that the Body of Christ will be edified and the unsaved led to the glorious light of the Risen Savior.

We are praying God's blessings on Pastor Bernard Smith, that He will bless you according to His Will and Purpose. **WE LOVE YOU!**

Blessings on You Always
The Workers

THE ENRICHED LIFE

Young people everywhere, be youthful and fruitful. Know the Lord Jesus Christ as your personal Savior. Start at home with a positive image of yourself and the community. Keep in mind the need to be kind for the person you meet on your way up; may be the same person you meet on your way down. Seek spiritual guidance.

Walk in the Way of the Lord and He will supply your every need. Grow in the Lord. Live a process of accountability, respectability and durability. Praise the Lord!

Lovingly,
The Authors

MOTIVATORS & INSPIRATORS

I am overjoyed with happiness to know that God has blessed you to begin writing your third book on "Spiritual Adventures."

May it be as successful as the others; may it be read nationwide so that others may know that you are a chosen vessel of God, bearing precious seeds of righteousness.

Starting at home with children to grandchildren and generation to generations. May the word of God have its desired effect for a better world for all people. Tell others about this woman inspired by God. I love you!

Your best friend,
Lillie B. Waters

Your previous books have been so well received; I am anxiously waiting to launch out in the deep. May God bless the reader and doers of the His Word.

Cartreen Ross

Your previous books have really inspired me and have given me a better understanding of God's will for my life through scriptures, history and poetry. Awaiting the new publication is exciting. We all love you!

Your niece,
Virdie Mae, Memphis, TN.

I have found Martha such an intelligent and interesting person, so caring to others; she is such an inspiration to others. I wish her well with everything in life and accomplishments.

Tina
Macomb, MI.

Having read your previous books, I am sure that God can and will make this one a marvelous success. God will make a great finish out of a slow start, especially if your heart is pleasing in His sight. Love you much. Blessings on you always.

Sister Thelma Fyfe

I am ecstatic to learn of the pre-publication of your third "Spiritual Adventures" book. The others were inspiring, enriching and should be placed in libraries across the nation but most especially utilized in the hearts of Christians. Until then we will gladly carry on.

Barbara McCorkle
San Diego, CA

I have found Martha's writings to be inspirational and insightful. Her continued writings show a spiritual depth that few others possess. I encourage others to reflect upon this book and allow the wisdom of these words to penetrate the soul.

Chaplain Ron Nitchie
Hospice of Michigan

I love Martha Brown! She has truly been an inspirational and well-rounded friend. Martha shares her humor and wisdom and has the Lord on her side. She shall always be remembered by those who love her.

Pat Schultz
Hospice of Michigan Volunteer

A RECIPE FOR A GODLY LIFE & LONGEVITY

Dear Aunt Martha,

Let me start by saying that you have had a very Positive influence on my life. You have always been larger than LIFE to me, or I should say us (my siblings). In your presence from my youth, when you entered into the room it was as if an Officer had entered, and I better be on my best behavior, and have the right answers if we were asked any questions. As I looked at your careers, as an Army Nurse, an Insurance Executive, and an Author, I learned that you may have as many careers as you like. Your example and my parents telling me I was as intelligent as anyone on the planet gave me the confidence to move forward.

This is a family, where failure is not an option. You are a part of the Village (family) that it takes to raise children; children of closely connected families have better success in life. When taught good moral values, we have a better chance to meld and endeavor to create a better society.

As a Successful Black Male that became a single parent of two successful children I have a few firsts in my career. Becoming the First Black Flight Medic for a Hospital Based Air Ambulance, I was not afraid to step out and do something different and have the confidence to say I am the best. I appreciate all the good Moral, Religious, Social, and Family values you and my Parents instilled in me. These are the same values that I tried to instill into my children.

There was never a direct connect between us but you being the successful Big Aunt (that was held in high regards by all of your siblings) gave not only me, but all of my siblings the knowledge that with the proper preparation we could be anything or anybody we set our minds on.

I can recall a conversation between me and my father on how to manage finances, he used your husband as an example to follow. I thought of both of you as the Ultimate Power Couple. Thank You for all of your influence and May God continue to Bless You.

Loving you!
Eddie Ishmael Jr.

Dear Aunt Martha,

I thank God for His loving kindness and tender mercy and permitting you to remain here for ninety years. Ninety good years! At this point you are anticipating the release of your book "Martha! Martha! The Third Spiritual Adventure." We love you! Congratulations!

But the fruit of the Spirit is love, joy, peace, longsuffering, gentleness, goodness, faith, meekness, temperance; against such there is no law. Galatians 5:22-23

Reverence D. Ishmael
and Family

Dear Aunt Martha,

May the Lord continue to bless you as a dedicated and anointed Christian educator. You have truly been an inspiration to me and many others throughout the world. It made me so proud in the 1990s when you allowed the Informer to publish one of your Christmas poems for my poetry section. We pray for the success of this publication.

With Love, Your Niece,
Mildred Madry Weatherspoon

SPECIAL ACKNOWLEDGEMENTS & GRATITUDES

Pastor Robert Smith, Jr., Pastor of the New Bethel Baptist Church, Detroit, having shared in the other editions, feels that this book will be more inspirational and motivating. We are praying for its success.

Pastor Puckett of the Green Grove Baptist Church, Detroit, has not read the previous publications but is waiting the third edition, "Martha! Martha!" Pastor Puckett has been a supporter of the family for many years.

Pastor Willie Thornton, Jr. of Mountain View Missionary Baptist Church, former Dean of Baptist Missionary Congress of Christian Education; your praiseworthy notations and admonitions to continue writing have been a great source of encouragement. I am deeply appreciative for your generous dissemination of information.

Blessings on my unyielding co-author, Freddie M Lindsay-Payne, whose devotion and sacrificial services have been paramount in my efforts. Thanks also to Payne-Pulliam School of Trade and Commerce, Inc., Detroit, Michigan for their labor of love.

Special thanks to Bernyce and Ted Sims for their consistency in communicating and travel from Akron, Ohio to Detroit. Thanks also to family for keeping up your loving concerns.

I wholehearted appreciate others whose keen insights have sustained me through the preparation and expedition of this third publication.

Delightful appreciation to author E.C. McKenzie for permission to use excerpts from his 1968 copyrighted publication, "1800 Quotable Quotes." Publisher, Baker House, Grand Rapids, Michigan.

Thank you for your gracious loving care…..Hospice of Michigan and Chaplin Ross.

American House – we are most grateful for team work and friendly attitudes. We are extremely grateful for all who shared in our recovery and our continual care. Some names to be remembered in the housekeeping department are: Tina Young, Crystal Morris, LaTrecia (Trecia) Kerksey, Ashley Allen, Christine Henzel and Gerald Davis, all from the Medical Team and on the move for our comfort.

The frequent use of the word we, has reference to my deceased husband, Granderson Brown who passed from this life at the age of ninety-eight great years.

IN MEMORY OF FAITHFUL SERVANTS

There are some who labored in the vineyard, relentlessly, and whose names are not recorded in our "Adventures", nevertheless they still live on in our hearts, minds and activities.

Association President Mattie Jackson, President of Women's Auxiliary Prospect District; VeElla Luckett, Superintendent of Sunday School; Reverend Macon Collins and Sister Martha Collins; Sister Irene Heard, Pastor Mellwood Brown and my wonderful husband, Granderson Brown deceased on August 20, 2011.

Author & Co-Author of the
Third Edition of Spiritual Adventures

ABOUT THE AUTHOR
MARTHA MAE ISHMAEL BROWN

Martha, the youngest sibling of Cary and Lula Ishmael, was born in Minter, Alabama on March 4, 1922. Later the family migrated to Pensacola, Florida where she graduated from the newly constructed Booker T. Washington High School as Salutatorian, Class of 1940. This class had one hundred and ten students of which there were four adult students. Their class motto: "We Stress Quality not Quantity." This has been Martha's theme for living abundantly in the Lord.

Martha studied at Bethune-Cookman College in Daytona Beach, Florida and Michigan Lutheran College in Detroit, Michigan. She also studied at Brewster School of Nursing in Jacksonville, Florida.

Martha was employed at Resthaven Hospital in Detroit; Detroit Receiving Hospital and Blue Cross Blue Shield of Michigan.

She was married to Granderson Brown, her wonderful husband, for over fifty years; they had no children but one adopted daughter, Freddie Lindsay-Payne; a precious niece, Bernyce Sims of Akron, Ohio and many nieces and nephews who have filled a void, especially now more than ever because of disability factors.

ABOUT THE CO-AUTHOR
Freddie M. Lindsay-Payne
As written by Martha Ishmael Brown

I would be remised if I did not introduce the co-author of this "Martha! Martha! Edition of "Spiritual Adventures" number three.

She is a long time friend of the family serving in the same local church for more than fifty years of which she was in the Missionary Ministry, chairperson of a Circle, "Aquila & Priscilla"; Church School Bible Adult Class Leader and instructor; Women's Day Speaker; educator: Business & Commerce and many others that I know not. I do know, however, that she is moving swiftly in both secular and religious activities.

Freddie is our long time friend, a Christ-centered person, a God sent person in whom the Holy Spirit dwells. She has ministered to me, personally, during my disabilities and my husband during his illness, who departed this life in 2011. She served spiritually and physically beyond the imagination.

Freddie Mae (Sweetie) is married to Mr. LeRoy E. Lindsay, a wonderful loving personality. Their knowledge and understanding of God and His will for them makes for a great husband and wife relationship.

To God be the Glory for this God "Child" and her husband.

May they be richly blessed to continue in the work of the Lord as doers, communicators and motivators.

ABOUT CO-AUTHOR
Freddie M. Lindsay-Payne

Mrs. Lindsay has 35 years of experience as a private career school owner and provider of vocational, employability and life skills training opportunities to persons desiring to enter into our employment society.

She is a member of Warren Avenue Missionary Baptist Church and has served her church and the surrounding community for over 50 years. She is directly involved in the Christian Education area of study and biblical concentration at Warren Avenue and district associations both locally and nationally.

Mrs. Lindsay is the former Dean of the Metropolitan District Congress of Christian Education. She has served in the capacity of Dean for the Prospect Baptist District Congress of Christian Education; in July, 2012, she was elected president of the Prospect Baptist District Congress of Christian Education. She is a Certified Dean through the Christian Education Department of Accreditation and Credentials, Sunday School Publishing Board, Nashville, Tennessee; June, 2005 she joined the faculty of the National Baptist Congress and taught in Houston, TX. Her managerial, professional and technical skills embrace people and organizations in helping to move projects and people forward.

Mrs. Lindsay has been a member of many organizations which include: Board member of the Michigan Association of Career Schools (MACS); board member of George Washington Carver Camp Association; past Chair of the Board of the High School of Commerce/East Commerce Alumni Association; past Chair of the Trustee Board and Chair of the Building Fund of Warren Avenue. Mrs. Lindsay has received numerous certificates, awards and commendations from public and private entities.

Mrs. Lindsay is married to Mr. Leroy E. Lindsay and has three adult children: Ronnelle Genora , Charles Maurice and one stepson Stephon Lindsay who resides in Gadston, AL. She has one very talented grandson Christian Floyd Payne who attends Southern University in Baton Rouge, LA.

Mrs. Lindsay contributes all that God has allowed her to be to her earthly parents, Deacon & Mrs. Garrett (Girlie) Hunt, her spiritual Mom, Mrs. Martha Brown, with whom she co-authors "Martha! Martha!, The Third Spiritual Adventure" and for whom she has much love and devotion because she demonstrated what God requires.

"To whom much is given, much is required."

General Themes

IS THE BIBLE REALLY TRUE?

Is the Bible really true? If so, what is truth? Webster's New Collegiate Dictionary describes truth as that which cannot be altered, changed, mixed or substituted. It is characterized by being in accord with what is not; what has been in reference to the past and what will be in the future. Truth transcends time and does not need to be proven or argued- but needs to be accepted. The Bible has been analyzed, criticized, ostracized and dogmatized; nevertheless, its divine essence remains fully inspired, stabilized and sanctified. This does not only apply to the written Word but also to the Living Word Jesus Christ, who proclaimed that He is the Way, the Truth and the Life.

The most profound truth and events in the entire Bible are found in the very first chapter of Genesis logically beginning at the first verse. "In the beginning God created..." When? No one knows. Where? Location unknown. What? Everything. Why? All things were created by Him and for Him. Colossians 1: 16, I have created him (man) for my glory. Isaiah 43:7b. How? For He spoke and it was done. He commanded and it stood fast (Psalm 33:9). The Lord hath appeared of old unto me saying (Jeremiah 31:3a), "Yea, I have loved thee with an everlasting love."

In King James Version, Genesis 1 has a total of thirty one verses; the word God appears thirty two times; in each of the first twelve verses once and in verse four twice. Is there any doubt how the universe came into existence?

There were no witnesses or media to record the events. Man's knowledge of the age of the planetary system is interesting and confusing; but indicative of a researching and inquiring mind. No one can testify beyond the shadow of a doubt the age of the universe; when time began or when it will end. People, places and things in constant motions are un- equivocal evidence of the Living God and the truth of His Word.

The Bible is truly fascinating. If the Word is studied frequently, meditated upon sincerely, one finds himself or herself profoundly interested in its contents. It is possible to be captivated or spellbound by some incidents, moved with compassion by subsequent events; baffled by others, enlightened by the Holy Spirit and increased in wisdom and knowledge.

Thy Word is true from the beginning: And every one of thy righteous judgments endureth for ever. Psalm 119:160. *The heavens declare the glory of God; and the firmament sheweth his handiwork.* Psalm 19:1.

These scriptures should impress upon the minds of potential readers the fathomable and unfathomable depth and beauty of the universe. That which we see with our eyes, touch with our hands, tread upon with our feet; explore with our minds; nurture within our hearts and feel within our beings are not just mere concepts of life but realities of the Eternal God and His infallible Word. Through the Word one should be convicted of his sinful nature, saved through grace by faith and the precious blood of Jesus.

For by grace are ye saved through faith; and that not of yourselves: it is the gift of God. Ephesians 2:8

SOME REALITY CHECKS OF BIBLICAL ORIGIN

1. God is Eternal, the Alpha and the Omega, Invisible but Omnipresent, Omniscient, Omnipotent and Immutable. He exists in a triune nature and is the Creator and Sustainer of heaven and earth. His name is to be exalted, magnified and His commandments obeyed. He is a loving God but will execute wrath and judgment according to His divine will. God is a Spirit and they that worship Him must worship Him in spirit and in truth.

2. The terrestrial and celestial heavens remain in constant orbit without man's ability to comprehend their full structure or controls.

3. Evenings and mornings continue as in the beginning. For the most part, the population still observes a seven-day week schedule; six days of work and one day to rest and worship. Seasons come and go in an orderly fashion or as God designates. Noah and his family were in the ark for approximately three hundred and sixty-five days equating to our present calendar year.

4. Man still has dominion over the earth and its creation; nevertheless, he has shirked his responsibilities shamefully.

5. The heaven of heavens remains a secret. The secret things belong to God. Deuteronomy 29:29.

6. Seas, rivers and bodies of water flow continuously. No more land has been added to the universe.

7. Egypt, Ethiopia, Damascus, Syria, Israel, Jerusalem, Asia, etc., still exist. Our modern day world expansions are all discoveries that were created in the very beginning.

8. Wars and conflicts prevail among Jews, Egyptians and Palestinians. Inherent rights to the land promised Abraham by God to his descendants set in motion a revolutionary condition created by Ishmael, the son of the bondswoman, Hagar, and Isaac, son of the freewoman, Sarah.

9. No one knows the date of creation. According to Biblical scholars, the best fixation of time dates back to the birth of Abraham in Ur of the Chaldeans approximately 2000-2500B.C. Archaeologists have uncovered evidence of Ur, where a high level of culture existed. In 1947, discoveries of the Dead Sea Scrolls have opened up new and valuable evidence on the preservation of ancient manuscripts.

10. The fulfillment of prophecies is living proof of the inspiration of the Bible to holy men of old. In Genesis 3:15, the first promise of a Savior to the world was made, repeated throughout the Old Testament and fulfilled in the New Testament; coming down through forty-two generations. Time dates were set into motion by the birth of Christ in the days of Herod, the King of Judea, dividing the Old Testament into Before Christ (B.C.) era and the New Testament in (A.D.) In the year of our Lord. (L. Anno Domini).

11. Secular history bears record to the life of Christ. Jesus Christ lived, worked, suffered, died on a cruel Roman cross, was buried and rose from the grave victoriously on the first day of the week bringing life, liberty, hope and salvation to all who believe (St. John 3:16). Because He lives we shall live also as we submit ourselves to His will and way.

12. Christ also prophesied the present calamities of this world in St. Matthew, Chapter 24. We are living witnesses of these prevailing conditions. The admonition is to remain faithful, prayerful and watchful for His imminent return to receive His own unto Himself.

13. The Sovereign God is constantly intervening in world's events to rescue wayward man from destruction of body, soul and mind. Jeremiah 31:3b. John 10:10b, "I am come that they might have life and that they might have it more abundantly."

The Gift of Love

Dear Friend,

How are you? I just had to send this letter to tell you how much I love you and care about you. I saw you yesterday as you were walking with your friends. I waited all day hoping you would talk to me also. As evening drew near, I gave you a sunset to close your day and a cool breeze to rest you and I waited. You never came. Oh, yes, it hurt me, but I still love you because I am your friend. I saw you fall asleep last night and I longed to touch your brow, so I spilled moonlight upon your pillow and face. Again I waited, wanting to rush down so we could talk. I have so many gifts for you.

You awakened late and rushed off for the day. My tears were in the rain. Today you looked so sad, so alone. It makes my heart ache because I understand. My friends let me down and hurt me many times too; but I love you. I try to tell you in the quiet green grass; I whisper it in the trees and leaves; I breathe it in the colors of the flowers. I shout it to you in the mountain streams and give the birds love songs to sing. I clothe you with warm sunshine and perfume the air. My love for you is deeper than oceans and bigger than oceans and bigger than the biggest want or need that you have.

We will spend eternity together in heaven. I know how hard it is on earth, I really know (because I was there) and I want to help you. My Father wants to help you too. He's that way, you know. Just call Me, ask Me, talk to Me. It is your decision. I have chosen you and because of this I will wait because I LOVE YOU.
Your friend,
Jesus

Author unknown–Received as a chain letter

RENEWING OUR COMMITMENT TO THE CHRISTIAN DOCTRINE

2 Timothy 4:1-5

In the second Epistle of Paul to his spiritual son, Timothy, there is an exhortation to faithfulness and complete commitment to the Christian Ministry of preaching and teaching. The latter portion of verse five reads "make full proof of thy ministry..." not 80% proof or 50% proof but full proof of thy ministry. This admonition is as timely today as it was when penned and should be applied by us in this turbulent society. I would like to project some personal questions regarding commitment for evaluation: (1) Am I making full use of whatever ministry the Lord has assigned to my heart and hands? (2) Am I agonizing, capitalizing, materializing, minimizing, scrutinizing or unionizing? (3) Am I serving with reluctance, with hypocrisy or with reservation? Now, if anyone finds himself operating within these negative categories, there is a definite need for renewal, a need for spiritual awakening or restoration.

Frequently there is an invitation for rededication of one's life to service. We ask if this is really necessary. Once truly dedicated should that suffice? This is a personal decision. The real answer lies in the possibility of broken covenants, broken commandments, willful disobedience or carnality. The children of Israel gladly and willingly accepted the commandments on Mt. Sinai saying, "...this we will do." Nevertheless, they constantly disobeyed. The plea from Almighty God was also constant; repent, return and be restored.

David felt the need to renew his broken relationship with God in Psalm 51. He cried out... "Create in me a clean heart O God; renew a right spirit within me. Restore unto me the joy of thy salvation; and uphold me with thy free Spirit."

Then will I teach transgressors thy ways; and sinners shall be converted unto thee." He wanted not only a renewal for himself but the same for others.

Restoration involves total revival bringing one's life into complete submission. It is that of loving the Lord God with heart, body, soul, mind, strength and neighbor as self. Love is the fulfillment of the law. Romans 13:10. When love has its free course life perspectives, goals and directions are changed.

Paul admonished Timothy to continue in the things he had learned with the assurance of knowing from whom he had learned them. Christian training in the home re-enforced by living examples are the most effective and influential devices in rearing children.

A story is told of a small boy who became quite frustrated at home because of parental discipline and decided to run away. He packed his little bag, threw it across his back and off to the streets he went. Soon he met an old man who recognized his unhappy disposition and inquired as to what was wrong. "Where are you going?" the old man asked. "I am running away from home," replied the boy. The old man made no attempt to stop him--just kept a watchful eye. Johnny soon made his way to a busy avenue where the exceptionally heavy traffic made it impossible to cross alone. Disgustingly he decided to return home. The old man said, "Johnny, what happened? You just told me you were running away." Johnny replied, "I was but I have always been taught never to cross the streets alone."

The implications are that there are times when we meet with problems, frustrations, disappointments and what have you on the busy highway of life without the necessary capabilities for solution. Seeking to run away may be impossible. However, there is consolation in returning home, remembering our roots and basic instructions. The plea is return, renew and be restored.

There are many commitments in life. We would like to mention at least three. (1) Commitments to equal opportunities, (2) commitment to service and (3) commitment to quality education.

As we consider the equal opportunities how happy we are for the "whosoever" teachings of Christ. The Bible has numerous references to man, every man; the multitude; the crowd; and the people. Truly God is no respecter of persons. We are all one in Christ Jesus. Nothing can excel the justice and equality of Christian teaching and essentially that of practical application.

Commitment to service is embodied in the life of Christ. Some well defined statements are: If any man serve me, let him follow me; and where I am there shall also my servant be. By love serve one another. No man can serve two masters... He who would be great among you let him become a servant. Because of some people's reluctance to be of service, they have not only failed in their commitment but also in effectiveness and leadership positions.

The commitment to quality education is stressed by many institutions of learning; nevertheless, there are numerous functional illiterates. Where is the advocated quality? Whom shall we blame? Thank God for the Christian doctrine that stresses both quality and quantity. It is not one of rhetoric but substance. It is not passive but active.

If one desires a dramatic change in his life style devoid of personal gratification, it is necessary to maintain an enrollment in the Institution of Christian Education. It was set in operation by the God of the universe, founded by the risen Christ and directed by the Holy Spirit. There can be no failures, no dropouts, no exclusions, no terminations, no bankruptcies, and no monetary fees or stipulations for increases. Accepting this challenge assures one of a life time membership in which he is constantly working on his eternal degree of being molded in the image of righteousness.

Are you making full proof of your ministry? Are you walking in the light of God's Holy Word? Do you know in

Whom you believe and that He will keep that which you have committed to Him? If so, then you can truly enjoin the hymnologist, Herbert Buffum, with the determination of "Going Through."

> Lord, I have started to walk in the light Shining upon me from heaven so bright. I bade the world and its follies adieu. I've started in Jesus, and I am going through. I'm going through. Yes I'm going through. I'll pay the price whatever others do. I'll take the way with the Lord despised few. I have started in Jesus and I'm going through.

THE INNER CONFLICT
Romans Chapter Seven

When we think of conflict, it is usually associated with disagreements in the areas of ideas, interests and opinions. Again, we may think of opposing forces of good and evil; right and wrong, strengths and weaknesses, struggling for the victory or possession of a particular object. How well do we know that the devil is busy waging war for the possession of men's souls? Someone has said that he kindles a tiny spark in the mind, fuels it by the lust of the flesh, supports it by the wind of prestige and recognition; keeps it alive by deceit and malice until it becomes uncontrollable, destroying lives and property. Conflict does not remain with the individual but projects itself without.

Chapter Seven deals with the frustration of the new walk – the flesh versus the Spirit or the old man Saul versus-the new man Paul. Walking in the newness of life as a babe is not easy. Sometimes stumbling, sometimes falling, sometimes reeling, sometimes rocking but as long as one is traveling toward the SON, the shadows are always behind him. Accepting the Lord Jesus Christ and His way of life does not immune one from temptations and suffering; in fact it is just the beginning of a diversified life.

There is an example of a man having had his purse stolen and later received a letter saying, "Sir, some years ago I stole your money. Remorse is gnawing me, so I am sending some back. When it gnaws me again; I will send more." This is manipulation of conscience or doing one's own thing. The godly way is to be led by the Holy Spirit. Let us examine some ways of resolving inner conflict: (1) By self examination, (2) identifying the problems and (3) by seeking deliverance and praising God.

I Corinthians 11:28 – But let every man examine himself. Upon examination, Paul made a startling revelation. He declared,

"I know that in my flesh there dwelleth no good thing, there is a willingness to do good but I can't find a way to perform it. When I want to do good, I don't; and when I try not to do wrong, that I do anyway."

Paul made a thorough examination of his weaknesses and strengths – so that from verses 14-25; the personal pronoun I is used 27 times, me and myself more than 10 times. You can readily see he had a problem and that problem was with whom? Himself.

It is wisdom to take an inventory of self. Open confession is good for the soul. Perhaps some people don't grow because they spend too much time blaming others for their shortcoming rather than learn from their mistakes. It is distressing how some people develop acute blindness about their own attitudes and actions while repeating the same offenses and remaining critical of others. Sometimes I find myself criticizing others until I reach my wits end. In order to justify my action, I indicate it is a healthy reaction, true and constructive. What about you?

Exodus 32:24, when Aaron was confronted by Moses concerning the golden calf he made for the Israelites to worship, he shifted the blame to the fire. So they gave it to me; then I cast it into the fire, and came out this calf. How incredible! How evasive! Blaming the fire, the environment, circumstances, ghetto, racial relation or any other factor for one's conflict is not the solution. There must be a desire to triumph.

In verse seven, Paul identifies the real problem. *Now if I do that I would not, it is no more I that do it, but sin that dwelleth in me.* This puts the blame squarely and honestly where it belongs. Sin, either that of commission or omission, is at the root of our failures and problems.

Parents must learn to identify conflicts and be responsible for proper discipline and training in the home. The sin of omission in some parents causes them to relinquish their duties resulting in erosion of family life and irresponsible young people. Instructions both religious and secular should begin in the home and extend to the communities, churches and schools. If left alone to grow, children may become negligent, delinquent, frustrated and released as question marks and time bombs into an already explosive, violent and fragmented society. Recognizing that behavior patterns are set by the time children reach school age, parents should do their best to assist them in developing balanced lives.

A little girl came in one day from playing telling her mother how extremely happy she was. Mother said, "I have never seen you so happy, why?" The child replied, "Well, I have been letting my thoughts toss me around. But today I tossed my thoughts around." Are you in control of your emotions?

Having examined self and identified the problem, at this point seeking deliverance is in order. Chapter Seven verse twenty four, *"Oh, wretched man that I am! Who shall deliver me from the body of this death?"* This is a miserable cry of one struggling to be delivered from the dead body of sin; old man Saul of Tarsus struggling with the new man Paul.

We are told it was the custom of ancient conquerors to tie a dead body to the backs of their prisoners to prevent them from escaping. Under these gruesome burdens and inhumane treatments the prisoners suffered physically and mentally. Inner conflict affects the well being of the total man making it impossible to run away.

If inner conflicts are not resolved they terminate into behavior problems sometimes necessitating counseling, psychoanalysis or psychiatric treatments.

A young man with a severe emotional problem had received therapy without significant result. Finally the psychiatrist discovered the real problem was the deep seated hatred he harbored for his father. "If I can identify the root of your problem would you be willing to apply yourself?" "Yes," replied the young man but when confronted with the need to become reconciled with his father, he flatly refused and walked out with his depression in tact.

People often become aware of their inner conflict and walk out on the therapy. Are you tied down to the dead body of resentment, envy, strife, hatred or any other evil condition?

If so, you need deliverance. Don't run out on the therapy of the Holy Spirit. Don't hold on to elements of destruction. All things being equal, the destroyer will win. Acknowledge your inability to deliver yourself from the bondage of sin and seek divine guidance. Inner conflict exists within the home, families, churches, auxiliaries, organizations and wherever there are people. It needs to be confronted squarely and honestly by self examination. We admonish you to call on the Lord in the day of trouble. He will deliver and to Him be the glory. Cry out in desperation for help. "Lord is it I? Am I a part of the problem or part of the solution?" Cry out as David did, "*Create in me a clean heart O God and renew a right spirit within me.*" Cry out as the publican, "*God be merciful to me a sinner,*" Cry out as the prodigal son, "*Father, I have sinned against heaven, and in thy sight...*" He will keep you in perfect peace if you trust Him.

THE TWO CONTROLLING SPIRITS

I John 4:1-3

Christians cannot deny that there are two unseen forces active in the lives of individuals controlling them for good or evil. Jesus Christ plainly said he that is not for me is against me. This opposition takes on many forms such as words, thoughts and actions. In a world of gross wickedness, alcoholism, drug addiction, sexual permissiveness, economic, political and social unrest, no one seems to have a valid answer or solution to any problem.

The Spirit of God is Preexisting - began with God, was on the scene before time and will reign throughout eternity. He is the Alpha and the Omega, the beginning and the end, the first and the last. Failure to accept the Preexisting Christ only shortchanges the individual and denies him the full benefit of an insurance written and guaranteed by God, payable on demand here and eternally sealed. There are no cancellations and no fine prints in God's plan of salvation.

The spirit of the antichrist began in time - some time prior to man's sin in the Garden of Eden; is permitted by God and will be terminated in due time by God at the second coming of Christ. The spirit of the antichrist began with a selfish motivation. Isaiah 14:12-14 is a record of Lucifer, the angel who was cast down to hell because of pride and rebellion. Five times I will is written. I will exalt myself, I will do this, that and the other, I will do as I please; I will set my own standards of living. These are unchristian attitudes seeking honor, position, vain glory and self satisfaction, rendering one ineffective for God's service. This doing one's own thing is described by Dr. Richard De Haan of the Radio Bible Class Periodical as Hedonist - strong will and head on down to destruction. *Pride goes before destruction and haughty spirit before a fall* (Proverbs 16:18). There is no right way to do a wrong thing.

Madelyn O'Hair is a typical example of the antichrist. Even though she calls herself a confirmed atheist, I have my doubts. Most Americans believe God exist, but their unwillingness to submit themselves to His authority to have their life styles changed is the greatest objection. Some people out of negative attitude of themselves, frustration, bitterness, revenge and inability to cope with internal and external situations seek attention in other areas in a negative manner to justify their inadequacies. He who rejects the Creator will create his own image to his own destruction.

Believers should be on guard against the antichrist. They should not be deceived into accepting ideas that are contrary to Biblical principles and revelation. Submit yourselves therefore to God. Resist the devil and he will flee from you (James 4:7). *"As many that are led by the Spirit of God these are the children of God."* We are constantly being reminded to shun evil and have no fellowship with any one who delivers any Gospel except that of Jesus Christ. You may identify the spirits as follows:

God is Almighty - antichrist is mighty. God edifies or builds up - antichrist destroys. God is Truth - antichrist is a liar. God is Holy - antichrist unholy. God is love, peace, joy, comfort and assurance. The leader of antichrist movement is the devil and the prince of the air. God is the Creator, Provider, Sustainer and Ruler of Heaven and earth with a kingdom that shall last forever and ever.

THE COMES OF DISCIPLESHIP

Many who confess that they have put on the badge of Christian discipleship and no longer dance to the drum beat of the world's music have developed some serious problems with the word commitment. Somewhere along the way, they have been misinformed side- tracked and missed the joy of service. On the contrary, others who have escalated their own joy, pursuing their happiness have lost the joy of knowing the Lord or never knew Him in the first place. When we speak of commitment, we are not concerned about spiritual ramification of sounding brass and tinkling cymbal which could easily generate an emotional high. For it does not matter how high you jump on Sundays but how straight you walk on Mondays. Commitment involves consecration, dedication, separation and transformation.

We can appreciate Webster's definition of commitment from the Latin word com-mit-tre, meaning to place one in custody of another; transference of one to a higher power for safe keeping. Examples: A patient committed to an institution or a criminal committed to a prison. My brothers and sisters, you may not consider yourself a patient needing care or a criminal needing protection; however, you need to be reminded that you were doomed to destruction had you not been rescued by our Lord. Indeed you were brought out of the darkness to the marvelous light of His love, delivered from the hands of satanic forces and transferred into the superior power controlled by the Holy Spirit. You are now safe, saved and sanctified.

It is a blessing to know that long before Webster came into existence our Lord and Savior Jesus Christ established the comes of commitment. He extended an invitation to Simon Peter and Andrew, his brother saying, *"Come ye after me and I will make you to become fishers of men"* Mark 1:17. To the unbelieving multitude, *"Come unto me all ye that labor and are heavy laden, and I will give you rest"* Matthew 11:28. Speaking of His critics and the wayward crowd, *"I am come that they might have life and that they might have it more abundantly..."*

The same invitation is extended today. Come, surrender, labor and receive the reward.

THE NEED FOR INCREASED LABORERS IN THE VINEYARD

Matthew 9:36-38

From this particular Scripture we find Jesus, the great Teacher, Preacher and Healer manifesting His divine power as He traveled through cities and villages. Upon seeing the multitudes of people who were scattered abroad, weak, helpless and seemingly lost as sheep without a shepherd, He had compassion on them. Just as Christ viewed this pathetic situation and spoke to His disciples about the need for laborers in the spiritual vineyard, He is speaking to us today.

When we think of children who are roaming the streets without adequate protection, direction or guidance, we know there is a need for laborers in the vineyard. When we think of adults misleading young people for personal gratification, we are more aware of the need and should be moved with compassion also genuine concern. Crime in our cities and nation should not only bring tears to our eyes and prayers on our lips but sincere desires to become involved.

When we think of parents neglecting their duties to children or broken homes and broken relationships, we should be moved by the words of Jesus Christ who said, *"Wist ye not that I must be about my Father's business."* (Luke 2:49). Frequently people think of laboring in the vineyard as working in the church serving on the usher board, auxiliary involvement and committee workmanship. These are mere church functions established for internal operation of the membership; but the real work of the church which all should be engaged in is <u>reaching others for Christ.</u> We come to church mainly to worship with heart, soul, mind and substance; then leave to go out into the world to serve our fellowmen.

Pastors are constantly reminding us through the inspired

word of our responsibilities. Yes, the harvest truly is white but laborers are few. Have you <u>lifted up</u> your eyes above fallen humanity or <u>looked on</u> them with compassion?

In order to be a laborer in the vineyard you must not only give of yourself in a self denial, sacrificial manner but of your substance likewise. Will you be a helper? Will you be a laborer? Can He count on you? The Lord has need of workers to till His field today. Has He led you to walk in wisdom's way? Will you respond in the language of the hymn, "O Blessed Savior Count On Me?"

FOUR TYPES OF WORKERS

A drifter as revealed in Ephesians 4:13-14 is one who has not come into the unity of faith and knowledge of Christ; he is tossed to and fro and carried about with every wind of doctrine and cunning tricks of men. He will react hastily at times without consideration; drift into unknown channels without direction and care less about reaching a goal. He will probably drift from one Church to another searching for something new instead of seeking for what is true. A remedy for this is to stir up the gift of God that is within one and commit one's self to the Lord and not unto men. In this you can be truly gifted and not drifted.

A Shifter is described in I Corinthians 10:12-13 *"Wherefore, let him that thinketh he standeth take heed lest he fall."* This person is overconfident about his position in Christ and when he is met with temptation, is unable to stand; will shift from one position to another to please others, lacking sound conviction; voting with the majority, compromising with the minority and swaying in the wrong direction for personal gratification. A remedy for this is to put on the whole armor of the Lord that he may be able to stand in the evil day.

The Shirker is found in Luke 9:57-62 where we read of those who express desires to follow Jesus but were unwilling to give up their families or way of life. They responded with excuses. Excuses rob one of the blessings and joys of a noble and richer life. Jesus said unto one of them, *"No man having put his hand to the plough, and looking back is fit for the kingdom of God..."* In Matthew 10:37-38, Jesus said, *"He that loveth father or mother more than Me is not worthy of Me; and he that loveth son or daughter more than Me, is not worthy of Me."*

It is time now to recognize the <u>Committed Consecrated</u>, full time Worker, survival of many spiritual battles; one who stands firm and tall with a fixed mind, an anchored hope and the blessed assurance of knowing the Lord. He is like a tree planted by the rivers of waters, fruitful, delightful and prosperous. He does not let his attitude prevent him from reaching the altitude the Lord has set forth for him and all who will remain faithful. The Committed Christian will carry out the ministry of Jesus, under the direction of the Holy Spirit, in the areas of preaching, teaching, healing, witnessing and ministering to the less fortunate. He will maintain his spiritual health by exercising daily and freely in the following manner:

Bend in humility, stoop in forgiveness; kneel in prayer; sit in meditation; rest in the Lord; reach out in love and walk in praise. Surely these strengthening exercises will prepare one for greater services and a fuller rewarding life. We should develop spiritual maturity; produce a more powerful light to those who walk in darkness and accumulate some extra grains of salt to help save a dying world.

> O God, open mine eyes that I may see The task that thou has given to me To do my best with all my might And look to thee for strength and light.
>
> I dare not think how I have shirked
> Or drifted away from thy manifold work
> Please forgive my failure, renew my mind
> Committed to thee, I would be thine.
> Forgetting myself and reaching for others I cannot see thee without my brother Just as I am I come to thee From selfish desires, please set me free.
>
> *Anonymous*

CHRISTIAN STEWARDSHIP
"Occupy Until I Come."
Luke 19:12-27

Generally speaking, a steward is one who manages the affairs or property for another during his absence and is accountable to the particular individual for all transactions. Just as a caretaker does not own the building he manages; or the cashier the money in the bank where he/ she is employed; or the guardian of orphans the property he holds in trust for them; so it is with the Christian . He is the trustee of God and holds everything in his possession as the Lord's and is subject to his sudden unexpected return to receive his own.

The concept of Christian stewardship begins with the Lord also ends with the Lord. Psalm 24:1 declares, *"The earth is the Lord's and the fullness thereof; the world, and they who dwell therein..."* This being true how then do we account for the possessive attitudes of some people? Perhaps, they have not learned the true meaning of stewardship.

This Scripture tells of a nobleman who went into a far country to receive for himself a kingdom. Before leaving he called together his ten servants and delivered a certain amount of money to each to invest and report on his return. The result was reward for those who invested wisely and condemnation for the slothful and wicked servant.

Our Lord Jesus is saying to us today, *"Occupy until I come."* He has invested a great deal in us and expects rich dividends in fruitful living. He expects us to redeem the time; to specialize in maximum instead of the minimum and to work while it is day for night cometh when no man can work. Christ has invested physical, mental and spiritual resources in us and expects all to be utilized. Time, talent and influence make up Christian Stewardship which culminates into a committed life. Are you willing to occupy until He comes?

Once an individual has put on the full badge of discipleship, there is no need to worry about his stewardship. Church membership is not discipleship. Showmanship is not discipleship; workmanship is discipleship, Christian discipleship involves learning of Christ as well as following examples and principles laid down by Him. The world is in darkness and filled with crime because Christians are looking to the prisons and other institutions, even the educational system to deal with the undesirable elements in our society. Prisons, reformatories and half-way houses are not substitute for transformed lives. It is our duties as stewards to reach out in these areas and occupy until He comes. The steward control life will give cheerfully and freely of the first fruit of his life because he recognizes the Lord as first in his life. Love destroys the seed of covetousness and selfishness.

CHALLENGE TO CHOOSE WISELY

Joshua 24:15

Joshua, the son of Nun, servant of the Lord and a strong leader labored patiently along with Moses to bring the children of Israel into Canaan is delivering his final speech. He is reminding this new generation of God's goodness and blessings. They were challenged to choose whom they would serve. Will you serve the true and living God in sincerity or the strange hand made idols of the surrounding nations? He reminded them that in spite of the fact they had experienced tremendous blessings, if they forsook the Lord, He would consume them. God's justice and retribution are as sure as His mercy. Joshua took a firm stand, *"As for me and my house we will serve the Lord."* What firm conviction without compromise!

I am wondering today how many leaders can speak not only for themselves but their entire family. I Timothy 3:5 informs us that if a man knows not how to rule his own house, how can he take care of the Church of God? Christians should be godly, wise and humble. They should possess strong leadership qualities which usually produce good fellowship. Just as the light of Christ shines in our lives reflecting itself to the world the same is true in the church and society. It is regrettable that some leaders in our churches are abusing the privileges of having been elected to leadership positions. They are advocating gambling, sexual permissiveness under the guise of sex education and many other God forsaken behaviors.

We are confronted daily with the task of many decisions. Some are of utmost importance and require deep concentration; whereas others require minimum thoughts and actions. Some people are more concerned about change of fashionable clothing than they are about dietary habits. Some are concerned about feeding the body instead of the soul. Some engage in transient moments of pleasure resulting in long time consequences. Some spend more time on material possession upkeep than quality time with children.

In a changing society where moral values are displaced by secularism, where parental influence has been diminished by conflicting laws of the land and local church leaders are seeking prestige, financial security and building fabulous structures, it is indeed high time to choose wisely. Whom will you serve? How will you serve? When will you serve? The challenge is to choose wisely; to seek first the kingdom of heaven and His righteousness and all other things shall be added. Matthew 6:33. We must never forget that what is right for us is right for our children. They are our most valuable resources. They must not remain functional illiterates. As the home and church go, so goes our society. Training, discipline and exampling lives are to be commended in all for it is better to see a sermon than hear one.

WE ARE GOD'S BUILDING

I Corinthians 3:9

For we are laborers together with God: ye are God's husbandry, ye are God's building. Paul is dealing with the immature Christians whose life styles of envy, strife, division and carnality had disrupted the unity of the body of Christ. He considered them to be babes in Christ unable to handle spiritual matters and the truth of the Gospel. Some had been influenced so greatly by their spiritual leaders that they were saying, "I am of Paul." Others were saying, "I am of Apollos" and still others were carried away by the preaching of Peter who was also called Cephas. In fact the Christians were centering their attention on men according to their intellectual abilities and spiritual wisdom instead of on God and Christ.

Here Paul condemns this division and proceeded to impress upon them the unity of Christ. He wanted them to know that as a missionary he had planted the Word of God in the hearts of the people; Apollos, as a minister of the Gospel came along and watered the seed; yet it was God who gave the increase. Therefore the important person is God and to Him be the Glory! You belong to God who is working in you, through you and for you. You are His building. Your allegiance should be to your owner. I am His and He is mine.

The message is as clear and valid today as it was during the first century. Ministers are servants of God entrusted with the message of salvation and are laborers together with God. They are to be honored and respected as leaders - not to be idolized as heroes of the Gospel or superstars of dramatic events. They are to direct saints into the path of righteousness and equip them for service. We belong to God. We are God's building.

In the construction of any building three fundamental factors must be considered: (1) The type of building to be constructed, (2) the type of material to be used and (3) the purpose of the building.

First of all we recognize the type of building as a living structure, a living body, a spiritual temple, a holy temple, a justified temple, a sanctified temple, a glorified temple, a graceful temple and a beautiful temple. Just as the Jews were concerned about the beauty of the temple in Jerusalem, so we must be concerned about the beauty of our souls utilizing the building blocks of God's eternal Word. Just as the city was fortified against the enemies, we are fortified by the grace of God. Just as Christ cleansed the temple casting out dishonest and unscrupulous merchants, He is cleansing lives today. He is still in the construction business - not in the demolition business. He is building, cleansing, restoring and repairing broken lives. We are His spiritual building. I Corinthians 3:16 *"Know ye not that ye are the temple of God and that the Spirit of God dwelleth in you?"*

Second factor is the type of material to be used. Most of you are familiar with the variety of temporary gifts given the saints such as apostleship, prophecy, teaching, evangelizing, healing, helper and others. However, since God is building for eternity, He permits us to have special building material in this life in order to prepare us for the eternal building not made with hands.

I Corinthians 13:13 *"And now abideth faith, hope and Charity, these three; but the greatest of these is charity."* These are the durable materials used. Faith comes first for without faith, it is impossible to please God. Hebrews 11:6 then cometh hope- not just wishful thinking but that blessed hope which keeps the building in tact followed by divine love that everlasting bond which cannot be eradicated by time, circumstances or conditions.

Third factor is designated purpose of the building. Man was made in the image and likeness of God for fellowship, for His glory and to have dominion over the work of His hand. Disobedience brought physical death - but thank God for spiritual life through Jesus Christ, our Savior. Thank God for molding us, making us, shaping and reshaping us, preparing us to enter our heavenly home without spot or wrinkle and blameless. Thank God for being the Architect; Jesus Christ the foundation and chief cornerstone. Thank God that the Holy Spirit, our Engineer and consultant keeps the building in perfect order. The crux of the whole matter depends on surrendering ourselves to His control.

A story was told of a coal miner's son who criticized his father severely concerning the manner in which he operated the family's business. One day the father left on an extended vacation permitting the son to exercise his expertise. Eagerly and over confident the son set out to master the business. Shortly after the takeover, problem after problem occurred without solutions. Each time the son sent a telegram to the father for help but without response. Finally a telegram came indicating the employees have struck and the coal mine was overflowing with water. "Please help me. What shall I do?" The father replied, "Use all of your personal credentials plug them into the outlet and maybe that will stop the flow of water."

There may be times in our lives when we are left alone to do our own thing because of our selfishness, strong will power and overconfident nature. Then we become a house divided against itself a building which cannot stand. Remember we are God's building and he forbids that we remain divided.

Let us recognize the workmanship of God. Let us be the city that sets on a hill giving light and direction to fellow travelers. Today is the day to hear His voice, to heed His word and to give Him your heart for an everlasting habitation. Give Him your division and He will give you His unity, Give Him your strife and He will give you His peace. Give Him your problems and He will give you His solutions. Give Him your all and He will answer your call. Give Him your house and He will make it a home. Give Him your emptiness and He will give you His fullness. Give Him your nothingness and He will give you His everything. Give Him your time and He will give you His eternity - a building not made with hands. Indeed we are God's building!

A SPIRITUAL AWAKENING
Lenten Season

"Why sleep ye? Rise and pray lest ye enter into temptation."
Luke 22:46

We are now into the observance of the Lenten Season according to our calendar commemorating the forty days, excluding Sundays that lead up to the resurrection of our Lord. It is the time that Christians everywhere should think seriously on the agony, betrayal, arrest, trial, denial, suffering and crucifixion of our Savior.

Those dark days of sorrow for Jesus and the disciples should remind us of the miserable and unprofitable days in our lives before the glorious sunrise of Easter burst forth that glorious light of salvation glowed in our souls. This should be a time of self examination, self denial, sincere worship, watchful outlook, forgiving spirits and prayerful attitudes.

Let us think now on the life of Jesus from the beginning; born poor that we might be rich; became a man but forever God; became a servant but Master of all things; help- less before the enemies but always Almighty and powerful.

Can you see Him with your mind's eye in the Garden of Gethsemane where He went to pray because his soul was exceedingly sorrowful even unto death? The weight of the world was upon his shoulders and He was alone in his suffering. Twice Jesus awakened his disciples, rebuked them for not being able to watch with him one hour while he prayed, twice He permitted them to sleep on and returned to his praying ground.

Sleep can be relaxing, refreshing, comforting and rejuvenating for succeeding events. However, it is sad indeed when Christians are sleeping instead of watching for the common enemy, the devil. The disciples should have been watching for the return of the Lord.

The third time Jesus came to his disciples He said, *"Why sleep ye? Rise and pray, lest ye enter into temptation. Rise let us be going; behold he is at hand that doth betray me..."* Today Jesus is calling us to wake up through his Word, through economic condition, through famine, earthquakes, wars, world unrest, turmoil within the church family. There is definite a need for spiritual awakening!

He would like you to wake up out of the sleep of sorrow. Cast all your cares upon him. Wake up out of the sleep of contentment and procrastination. Now is the appointed time. Wake up out of the sleep of retaliation. Vengeance is mine, I. will repay, said the Lord. Wake up out of the sleep of hypocrisy, overconfident and lip service. Take heed lest ye fall also like Peter and others.

Once we are awake, we are admonished to remain awake; not to turn over again but wake up and get up. Jesus knows when we have slept enough. Therefore he bids us rise up, stay up, stand up, dress up, speak up, give up and work up.

Before taking off, take time to pray. Jesus prayed frequently and sincerely so that sweat was, as it were great drops of blood fell down to the ground. As the angel ministered to Jesus so will the Holy Spirit minister to us and strengthen us.

There is no greater need than to follow our Savior. Follow him through the garden though it appears beautiful physically; there may be many hours of sorrow and depression awaiting you. Follow him through the enemy territory being careful not to warm oneself at the devil's fire. Follow him to Calvary for it was there He uttered the words, "It is finished," as He died for you and me. Follow him to the grave and rise with newness of life. If we suffer with him we shall reign with him.

THE RESURRECTION

Our theme is taken from the four Gospels account of our Lord's resurrection and the devoted women coming to the tomb early in the morning with spices to anoint His body as was customary in those days; not only because of the custom, but out of deep affection for the Master. He ministered to them during His life and they had come for the finally burial ceremony.

The Holy Spirit directed these writers to tell the Good News of our Lord using different approaches, styles, dramas, and order of events; therefore care must be taken to evaluate them only as the Holy Spirit dictates in order not to call them contradictions.

Let us take a brief look at the Gospel Writers. Matthew, Mark and Luke's writing are called the Synoptic Gospels because they follow a common pattern in relating some of the same events on the life and ministry of Jesus. Matthew appealed more to the Jews, presenting Jesus as King of the Jews. Mark appealed more to the Romans, stressing the power of Jesus; using the word straightway frequently. Luke, the physician and historian leaned toward the Greeks; emphasized Christ's concern for lost humanity; detailed His compassionate nature for the sick, mistreated, bereaved; and included the ministry of women to Jesus.

John's Gospel is a supplement to the other three giving new and deeper insight into the life and Spirit of Christ. He presented Christ as the Great I Am, and often made use of the words, love, believe, truth and witness. John seemed to have summarized the message of the others in John 20:31. *"But these are written that ye might believe that Jesus is the Christ, The Son of God and that by believing ye might have life through His name."*

John, the beloved disciple was so impressed with the loyalty of Mary Magdalene, the woman out of whom Christ had cast seven devils; that he devoted a great deal of the 20th chapter of St. John to her face to face encounter with the risen Lord. He did not mention the other women at all, however, the Synoptic Gospel

Writers recorded that they had gone to tell the Good News to the disciples when Mary returned to the empty tomb. In her loneliness and grief stricken moments, Christ revealed himself unto her. She did not recognize him at first but when He called her by name, her heart rejoiced and she wanted to embrace him. Jesus rebuked her and said unto her. *"Touch me not; for I have not yet ascended to my Father. But go to my brethren and say unto them, I ascend unto my Father and your Father and to my God and your God."* In other words, don't detain me now; I am on my way to present my body to my Father, but you hasten to tell the news to the disciples, my brethren. Don't seek to hold me on the earth, but become a messenger of new joys. The disciples neither believed Mary nor the other women, to whom He appeared later that day. Luke said their words seemed as idle tales.

    Never worry if people don't believe you, after all many did not believe Jesus Christ. In spite of doubt, continue to tell the story; tell it with courage and conviction; in songs, praises, and most of all, with a changed life!

CHRISTIAN REJOICING IN COMMITMENT

Chapter twelve of Paul's letter to the Romans is of tremendous importance because it contains wholesome and in-depth instructions regarding Christian dedication and service involving the total personality; the body, mind and spirit. We would like to center our attention on (1) Rejoicing with consecrated bodies, (2) Rejoicing with consecrated minds and (3) Rejoicing under the control of the Holy Spirit.

Rejoicing with our bodies is a daily commitment. If you would eliminate migraine headaches during the day, start in the morning getting your head on straight by presenting it to the Lord. Bow in submission to His will, thanking him for the day and seeking his guidance all the way. Let him remove the spiritual cataracts from your eyes as you sing, "Open Mine Eyes" that I might see, glimpses of truth Thou hast for me. He will in turn remove the deafness from your ears as you listen to the voice of Jesus calling, Who Will Go and Work Today? Your nostrils must be presented by all means permitting him to clear your nasal passage of being heavily involved in other people's business. This being done, you are now prepared to inhale life's sustaining oxygen necessary to vitalize every cell of your body. Let him breathe on you His abundant life.

With the toothbrush of His love, He is waiting to brush away the foulness of your mouth; improving your taste buds, enabling you to taste and digest the Word of God with Ease. Oh taste and see that the Lord is good. Blessed are they that trust in him! Now you are ready to sing praises to His name without worrying about ten thousand tongues, simply praise Him with the one you have in sincerity and truth. Praise Him as you sing "Glory to His Name." Let him make something beautiful out of your life.

In order to partake of the abundant life, your body must be washed in His goodness and cleansed by His love before you can dress up in His righteousness. Christians are admonished to put on proper clothing as described in Ephesians, Chapter 6. Fashions that are too revealing or too extreme should be avoided by all means. Never cast your pearls before swine in dress or action.

What about the extremities? O what problems we have with aching joints! The Lord is able to remove the arthritic conditions as you exercise. Exercises improve the circulation both physically and spiritually. Stretch forth your right hand rejoicing, "Father I Stretch My Hand To Thee." With the left hand you are in a position to do what He wants you to do; "Rescue the Perishing," care for the dying, snatch them in pity from sin and the grave; weep over the erring one, lift up the fallen, tell them of Jesus the mighty to save. Reaching out to others is the most rewarding aspect of the Christian life. The mission of the Church is an outreach rather than pacifying those within the fold. Keep your arms out... be careful not to get your elbows too comfortable leaning on the everlasting arms that you forget to "Stand Up For J-E-S-U-S, JESUS!"

What physical defects you have and infirmities may be compensated by utilizing your mental faculties to the glory of God. Stand on His Promises and Walk in the Path of Duty! Rejoice! Rejoice!

Rejoice with consecrated minds. In verse two we read: and be not conformed to this world; but be ye transformed by the renewing of your mind. An addition to this is II Corinthians 5:17, "*...therefore, if any man be in Christ, he is a new creature; old things are passed away; behold all things are become new.*" One of the most besetting problems in the Church family today is that too many people are mentally disturbed. Their minds are still focusing on carnal affairs, money, prestige, infidelity and idolatries of various natures. The Holy Bible has been tossed aside and ungodly men are forcing their own doctrines, rules and regulations on immature minds. No wonder we have so much spiritual revolution and violence in the Church.

To keep your mind in the right perspectives, start your day singing "Woke up this morning with my mind stayed on Jesus." If your mind is stayed on Jesus, He will keep you in perfect peace with a song of thanksgiving ringing in your heart. If your mind is stayed on Jesus, He will balance your split personality enabling you to be humble, forgiving, obedient, prayerful and submissive. If your mind is stayed on Jesus, you may be able to say, "Speak Lord for they servant heareth." If your mind is stayed on Jesus, you will be careful about giving someone a piece of your mind for fearing you may not have enough left to get along with. If your mind is stayed on Jesus, He will remove your guilt complex, empowering you to withdraw from worldly activities and enable you to be like Him. If you mind is stayed on Jesus, He will bring you out of your depression and lift you up as you "Lift Him Up." Then you can truly sing with a lively hope, "I'll Be Like Him," "I'll Overcome" - and "I'll Be All Right." Rejoice! Rejoice!

If you would enjoy the blessings and deep secrets of a happy life; body, mind and spirit; follow the principles laid down in the Bible. Study the lives of those from the Old and New Testaments who were not controlled by external circumstances but by faith. Permit me to paraphrase a hymnology concerning the prophet Habakkuk's state of happiness from Habakkuk 3:17-18. I shall not be moved even though the fig trees don't blossom, and the Lord wills it so that I am deprived of fruit; or my labor is in vain so that the fields are barren and I am left without food. I shall not be moved if the cattle don't come home, or the pigs go astray or the stalls are empty. In spite of this I am going to praise the Lord for He is the joy of my salvation. Is He the joy of your salvation? Let nothing deter you from shouting Hallelujah! Blessed Assurance!

If you would remain happy, it is necessary to maintain a permanent enrollment in the Institution of Christian Education. It was set in operation by the God of the universe, founded by the Risen Savior and directed by the Holy Spirit. There are no failures, no dropouts, no exclusions, no terminations, no bankruptcies and no monetary fees required. Accepting the challenge assures one of a lifetime membership in which he is constantly working on an Eternal Degree of being molded in the image of righteousness.

RECOGNIZING THE FRUIT OF COMMITTED LIVES
Women's Day Address

Romans Chapter Sixteen

In this Chapter, Paul closed his letter to the Church at Rome with some of the most beautiful expressions of loving concern and appreciation for the ministries of dedicated workers. About twenty six personalities are recorded of which many were Paul's personal friends having previously ministered to his needs. Others were relatives, some unnamed; but all received his salutations, recognition and gratitude. What is most impressive and interesting is that women received top rating.

The names of outstanding women comprised more than one third of the entire roster. This selection was not by chance but based on service and does not support the theory of some that Paul was anti-women. Indeed he commanded the women to keep silent in the churches at Corinth, to be obedient according to the laws and if they would learn anything ask their husbands at home. What if there is no husband? What if there is a husband and he is not knowledgeable in the Word of God? Surely the Lord has not left himself without a witness. There is usually available a pastor, minister or godly believer to give spiritual guidance. Women, it is needless to worry since the Holy Spirit has His own way of teaching and reaching individuals. Meanwhile, being a single person may provide tremendous opportunities to devote more time to the Lord's work.

Now let us focus our attention on some of those receiving recognition for their fruitful living: (1) A dedicated servant, commonly known as a deaconess, (2) a noteworthy husband-wife evangelistic team, (3) sisterhood of willing workers and (4) a godly mother. Naturally Paul would direct his attention first of all to Phoebe, a devout woman, from whose ministry he had benefitted and who had accepted to hand deliver his letter to the church at

Rome. Can you imagine a woman letter carrier in those days? Women have made a profound impact on the spread of the gospel throughout history. Paul recommended Phoebe highly to the Church as our sister, a servant in her own local Church and one who specialized in helping others. He entrusted her to their care, requested that they receive her in the Lord as becometh saints and assist her in <u>whatsoever business</u> she had need of. What a powerful statement!

We turn now to the husband-wife evangelistic team or should we say the wife-husband team since Priscilla's name is written before her husband, Aquila? Many scholars have asked why? We do not know why, however, we accept the fact that all Scripture is written by the inspiration of God and is always profitable. What is not known to men is eternally known in heaven. Of the six times their names are recorded in the Bible, they are not written separately but together. Three times Aquila's is placed first and the remaining three times Priscilla or Priscae's first. These two were in cooperation with each other <u>not</u> in competition with each other. Does this remind you that woman was created as a help meet for man? A bone was removed from Adam's rib and not his head or his foot.

Paul's relationship with this couple was exceptionally close; living together on occasions, working together as tentmakers; traveling together as fellow laborers in Christ and facing persecution together. He was generous in his recognition of them and felt indebted to them because they risked their lives for him.

Have you risked anything of value so that the Gospel of Jesus Christ may have its fruit among others?

One cannot excel the togetherness of this team; one in the Lord, one in marital bliss, one in their friendship with Paul; one in secular occupation and one in using their spiritual gifts of teaching and evangelizing. In the final analysis we are told they were martyred together for the cause of Christ. Till death do you part! An amazing marvelous life together! I am wondering how many here today long for a similar relationship and strive to attain it. It's a real challenge!

The United Sisterhood of Willing Workers consists of those noble dedicated women, who exercised their God given talent, time and influence for the cause of Christianity. After hearing the Word, they answered gladly saying here am I, send me, as they moved out from the comfort of their homes to vineyards of service in a self-sacrificial manner. Recorded in verse six is Mary of Rome, who labored much assisting Paul and his companions. Verse twelve Tryphena and Tryphosa believed by some to be twin sisters were also tireless workers; followed by Persis, described as beloved and one who labored abundantly. Salutations were extended to Nereus's sister and all the saints in the church. No one was excluded. They heard the word, understood the word and brought forth much fruit; some a hundredfold, some sixty and some thirty according to the work of the Holy Spirit; but most important they were all fruitful. Note the frequent references to the words help and labor... these should be a constant reminder of our Christian duties to be laborers and fruit bearers; not bearers of wild fruit but that which is properly cultivated and nourished.

Thank God for the dedicated lives of the sisterhood of believers and godly mothers who refuse to sit under their own vines and fig trees basking in their own importance while sons and daughters travel the road to destruction. Thank God for those who refuse to center their attention on designer's clothing, material fads and high fashions but on the Master Designer, Creator and Sustainer of all things. Thank God for those who seek to direct the members of their families to the Rock; the Rock of all Ages; the Rock that does not shake, rattle or roll. Thank God for young people who dare to be different and whose value system is not based on the world's standard. Thank God for those who refuse to cast their pearls before swine knowing that they will trample them under their feet. Thank God for all who are a source of inspiration to others; for the innumerable contributions of women in every generation, in every walk of life; young and old, rich and poor; great and small; black and white...all are precious in His sight.

Recognition is now given to a godly church mother, unnamed but described in verse thirteen as the mother of Rufus and mine. This phraseology seems to be that of a spiritual adoption. Who was Rufus? Paul called him chosen in the Lord. Rufus was also one of the sons of Simon, a man of the African country of Cyrene; who was coming out of the country during the Passover season when forced by the Roman soldiers to bear the cross of Jesus as he climbed the rugged hill to Calvary. The two sons of Simon, Rufus and Alexander along with their mother became members of the Christian community. How heart warming it is to have someone adopt your mother as his or her own. Adopting a godly or spiritual mother by a child or adopting a child by a godly mother should be greatly encouraged. One cannot over emphasized teaching and training in the home using the Word of God, the Ten Commandments, the Model Prayer, the Sermon on the Mount or the Beatitudes, but above all stressing the importance of being doers of the Word and not hearers only. Paul did not want the Church to lose her fruitfulness and the joy of knowing the Lord.

In conclusion, the challenge is to every man, woman and child who has committed himself or herself to the Lord to be fruitful and watchful. We admonish those who have not accepted Jesus Christ as their personal Savior to hear, believe, confess your sin and trust Him who is a new and fulfilling life. In order to bear fruit continuously, your life must be cultivated with the Word of God empowered by the Holy Spirit, pruned with prayer and watered with loving kindness. The question is where is the fruit of your life? Where is the fruit of your life as a minister, a deacon, a deaconess, evangelist, missionary, mother or a born again believer? Are you remaining in one place withering away? Has the Lord plucked you up? Have you any fruit for the hungry? Anything for the thirsty? Have you any goodies that will spill over into the life of a child? Where is the fruit of your life?

Remember the words of Jesus, *"Abide in me and I in you as the branch can not bear fruit of itself, except it abide in the vine; no more can ye except ye abide in me."* Oh the rich blessing of abiding in the Lord is like the tree that's planted by the rivers of water that brings forth his fruit in his season; his leaf also shall not wither and whatsoever he does shall prosper.

THE WOMAN WHO BROUGHT OTHERS TO JESUS

St. John 4:28-29

The Apostle John spared no pain delivering to us the whosoeverness of God's plan of salvation, chapter four exposes us to the acceptance and faith of a Gentile woman in bringing others to a saving knowledge of Christ. Through this despised woman, social, racial, religious and sexual barriers were broken down also the true meaning of worship established. St. John 4:24.

She was made in the image and likeness of God consisting of body, mind and soul. Therefore, we shall attempt to discuss what she was like physically, intellectually and spiritually.

What was her physical composition? She was a despised Samaritan, hated by the Jews because she was racially mixed (part Jewish and part Gentile). In 722 B.C., according to Biblical history, the Northern kingdom was invaded and captured by the Assyrians who took the stronger, healthier and more affluent people out; especially the men and brought in foreigners to inhabit the land, to keep peace and to cohabit with the weaker Jews. This created a mixed race of people called the Samaritans; hated, despised, and considered the underdogs by Judah, the Southern kingdom which remained a purer race. After seventy years of captivity by the Chaldeans in Babylon, return and rebuilding of the temple in Jerusalem, hostility continued until the coming of Christ.

This woman was lonely, bearing her burdens in the heat of the day. She came to the well alone probably because of her reputation as a woman of many husbands. It is a well-known fact that life is sometimes lonely, but in your lonely hours you never know what God has planned for you. I declare that if you meet Him at the well, He'll walk with you. He will talk with you also tell you what you need to know and show you even more.

You need to know she was a busy woman carrying a water pot to draw water. Jesus is calling busy people to a life of service;

not to a sedentary life style. The harvest truly is ripe but laborers are few. Can He count on you?

She was a special interest person. Jesus had a special interest in her and she also had interest in Him. There was an attraction that went beyond visual recognition to the display of intrinsic values of the soul. All of God's children have this attractiveness which needs to be refined and displayed. Hers was a sacred trust reserved for her only. No wonder Jesus said, *"I must need go through Samaria."*

He had a special appointment with a special woman. Time, 12:00 noon, where? Jacob's well in the village of Sychar just outside Samaria. The purpose was to break down the hostility which existed between Jews and Gentiles. The disciples were not equipped to do this since this was during Christ's early ministry. Even when Christ sent them out later, they were not to go into the way of the Gentiles nor enter into any city of the Samaritans.

From an intellectual standpoint, she was knowledgeable, responsive, alert and tactful. She possessed the ability to handle situations wisely without offending others. She knew how to be evasive in matters of personal involvement. When asked about her husband she made an honest confession, *"I have no husband."* Shortly afterward she changed the subject to one of worship.

Intellectually, she knew the history and heritage of her family, claimed Jacob as her father in spite of her Gentile background, had searched the then known Scriptures and looked forward to the coming of the Messiah.

Morally, she was a sinner living in adultery having had five husbands, and then she heard the word of Jesus, believed in her heart that he was the Messiah, confessed her sins, had a change of attitude and became a living witness.

This woman was a remarkable communicator. It has been said that if you want to get a message over; telegram, telephone or tell a woman. This ordinary woman became an extraordinary channel of communication more sophisticated than Ameritech. No waiting period, back-up lines, technical difficulties, personnel problems, direct person to person contact and most of all no charge for service. Her challenge of a personal invitation to meet Jesus for themselves was accepted.

That woman who brought other to Jesus could be you, or you. You could be involved in a missionary outreach.

> Come regardless of physical,
> intellectual or moral conditions.
> Come empty, and feel His existence
> Come sowing, go away reaping
> Come lame, and bear no blame
> Come sad, and He'll make you glad.
>
> Come in unbelief, faith will give you relief
> Come mourning, there will be no scorning
> Come hating, and leave loving... !
> Come as a sinner and leave as a winner
>
> Come as a man, and take a stand
> Come without friend,
> He'll be with you to the end
> Come seeking his face, and receive grace
> Come in despair, He is always there
>
> Come without bread, and leave well fed
> Come desiring a drink, He'll lead you to think
> Come caring, and leave sharing
> Come give Him your all, He'll answer your call.

LIVING IN A WARRING SOCIETY

We must confess that we live in a warring society that is constantly changing from one thing to another. There are wars and rumors of wars, nation against nation, kingdom against kingdom, husbands against wives, wives against husbands, parents against children, children against parents. There are wars and conflicts of all descriptions: civil, domestic, foreign, religious, intellectual, psychological, moral, social and economic. Indeed we live in an age where things are going from bad to worse, from worse to seemingly a state of moral and spiritual bankruptcy. We live in an age where truth is forever on the scaffold and wrong on the throne. We live in an age where wrong is highly publicized, magnified and glorified, whereas right is criticized, penalized, victimized and often crucified. These are indeed troubled times. In homes, parents have accepted a subordinate role in the rearing of their children or possibly no role at all. Child care organizations and foster homes are increasing at an alarming rate, mainly, to care for the neglected, abused and indigent. No wonder there are so many high school drop- outs, drug abuse drop-ins, street casualties, young people missing in action and regretfully older people willfully misleading and incriminating the young.

What about wars on the religious front? Do you not know that there are about as many aristocrats and religious diplomats in the membership of the local church as there are crooks in the political arena? I said in the membership, not in the Body of Christ. The quest for position, one to sit on the right hand and the other on the left is greater than the willingness to serve. There is an ever present question as to why there are so many wars. First of all, because Jesus said so in Matthew 24:6, *"And ye shall hear of wars and rumors of wars: see that ye be not troubled: for all these things must come to pass, but the end is not yet..."* James, Chapter 4, tells us that wars come from lust and greed within us desiring that which we cannot afford. The reason we don't have is because of the whole army of evil desires within us trying to satisfy our own pleasures.

Even if we pray, God does not answer our prayers because of wrong motives (Romans 1:21).

> *"Because when they knew God, they glorified him not as God, neither were they thankful, they became vain in their own imaginations and their foolish heart was darkened. Professing themselves to be wise, they became fools. Wherefore, God gave them up to do their own thing. Yet we have no excuse for our actions."*

Even the world is saying to the Christians, "get your act together."

Now, what are the solutions? Jesus Christ, the Prince of Peace, has already armed the believer with the necessary weapons to silence the enemies and relieve the troubled mind. Matthew 6:33; *"but seek ye first the kingdom of God and His righteousness and all these things shall be added unto you."* John 10:10, *"I am come that they might have life and that they might have it more abundantly."* Ephesians 6:13 says, *"Wherefore, take unto you the whole armor of God that ye may be able to stand in the evil day."* Christ is the answer.

THE PEACEFUL ROLE OF WOMEN IN SOCIETY

What steps should be taken when one finds herself in a distressful or warring situation? In the business world, when one finds himself stressed out with liabilities exceeding his assets he usually seeks counseling or enters into a bankruptcy preceding called Chapter 11. Women, you have no need to wait until you are spiritually or morally bankrupted. Get into Chapter 11 - now. Consult the D.A. What do you mean by the D.A.? Consult the Doctrine of Affirmation. Get into the 11th chapter of the epistle to the Hebrews, better known as the Faith Chapter. Begin with God. Hebrews 11:6, *"For without faith it is impossible to please Him; for he that cometh to God must believe that He is and that He is a rewarder of them that diligently seek Him."*

Briefly, we shall attempt to scrutinize a few passages in Chapter 11 to discover some of the contributions women made to peace. The Political arena, verses 23-24 we find the parents of Moses defying the decree of King Pharaoh, who charged that all Egyptian sons that were born be cast into the river, and all daughters be saved. We must admire the spiritual maturity of Jocabed, the mother and the strategy she and Miriam, the daughter, used for the protection of the child. Believing that God was able to save and protect the child brought peace to the family and gave to the world one of the greatest leaders in Biblical history. Wish there were more mothers like Jocabed who would build a wall of protection around their children to save them, not only from government ungodly rules and regulations but from substances detrimental to their health and well-being. Parents should learn to have strong convictions, impress righteous principles through examples upon their children and teach them to stand up for right rather than fall for anything. In our society Clementine Barfield, the organizer of Save Our Sons And Daughters (SOSAD) is a living and excellent example. There are many other concerned parents.

Social and Moral arena: Hebrews 11:31 tells of Rahab, the

harlot, whose life and the lives of her family were saved because she received the spies with peace; believing they were directed by God, who had wrought mighty works in their lives. Rahab became an ancestor of Christ through the lineage of David. God can take the most wretched individual and transform that life into a most beautiful vessel. When the WORD OF GOD convicts us of our sinful state of being, we should be concerned about others especially members of our family.

Let us consider the third aspect of contribution in verse 32 which tells of Barak's faith; however it is feasible to review the records of the Judges in Chapter 4 to link his action up with that of his associate. Let me present to you this most dynamic feminine leader, a judge, a prophetess, a wife, a poetess, a career woman for the Lord, a great spiritual giant and physical warrior - Deborah. As the fourth judge of Israel, she sent for Barak (who became the fifth judge) to make an inquiry of him. She said, *"Hath not the Lord commanded you to take troops and go toward Mount Tabor and I will deliver Sisera unto thine hand?"* Barak did not respond with a yes or no; however, he did say to Deborah, *"If thou will go with me, then I will go; but if thou wilt not go with me then I will not go."* She answered, *"I will surely go with thee but the honor will not be thine for God will sell Sisera into the hand of a woman."* This is the Spiritual arena.

Note the peaceful relationship that existed even when it seemed that the woman's faith excelled that of the man's. When the Lord gave them the victory, together they lifted up their voices in praises to the God of their salvation. There is always room for doing the right thing and compromising. By developing a strategy in dealing with the conscientious objector, you may win both the war and the peace. Each person has a contribution to make to society which he alone can do. Do not crush the other person; after all God made woman as a help meet to man (Genesis 2:18). What is wrong with helping him to meet the need in any arena? Use your faith and God given wisdom to the glory of God whether you are accepted or not. To God be the glory!

I would like to remind you of a story I heard of a man who had two matches; he lost one in the dark, struck the second to find the first; leaving him with nothing and still in the dark. To those who do not have the match of God's love and the flame of peace within your hearts, it would be a terrible mistake to come to the end of your journey in this life to be cast out in utter darkness. Christ can and will bring you out of the darkness to the marvelous light of His love.

YOUNG PEOPLE'S ROLE IN SOCIETY

Young people should consider themselves fortunate to be living in a push button, streamline and highly scientific age. Life spans are increasingly longer, people may remain in the work force and be useful citizens as long as they desire or their health permits. In spite of glorious opportunities to live and let live, religious freedom, educational advantages and counseling programs: crime, disrespect, hard core unemployment are ever-present problems among young people. It is unfortunate that open rebellion is outrageous in some.

Many youth have encountered difficulties in the early stages of their lives due to broken family ties, little or improper home training, no Christian background, misguided lives and following the wrong crowd.

As a child, one is totally helpless in a home where there are no prayers, no grace at mealtime and no faith in a living God. However, we as Christians can demonstrate what we have been taught, tell others about Christ as our personal Savior and invite them to Church and Sunday School.

Young people can be kind, thoughtful, loving, helpful, obedient and truthful. Learn to stand up for right regardless of the consequences. They should become involved in constructive activities and concern for all people. These are not easy but with continuous Bible study, prayers and Christian fellowship, they will make it. Most certainly, with attentive parents, God-fearing leaders and Christian guidance, the victory is already won. Realistic goals and godly standards are essential to true happiness.

CHRISTIAN PARENTS COMMENDED

Paul recognized and thanked God for special Christian training that had been instilled into the life of Timothy by his mother, Eunice, and grandmother Lois. Here you will find three generations commended. Grandmother passed on to her daughter godly principles; daughter planted the seed of righteousness into the life of her son; and the son received the instructions so well that he was converted at an early age and was profitable to Paul in the ministry (II Timothy 1:5-6).

As Paul admonished Timothy so mothers and daughters should impress upon the mind of the young to stir up the gift of God that is within them. The Holy Spirit will empower and direct the believer into service. A good start is fine but zeal and faithfulness are rewarding factors.

Paul's letters indicated certain Christian qualities were reflected in the life of Timothy and worthy of emulating. The qualities are those of being lovable, teachable, flexible, responsible and reachable. We will touch on them lightly.

The nature of being lovable is found in Paul references to Timothy as my son, my son in the faith and my dearly beloved son. Some younger people find many objections to developing friendship with older people and vice versa. Out of love each should seek better relationship, not as buddies, but to enrich each other lives and make society a better place in which to live. The love of God constrains us to do this.

As far as being teachable is concerned Paul's letters to Timothy are overflowing with instructions for himself, the Ministers, Deacons, women and the general operation of the Church of the living God. Parents and children should keep open and receptive minds as each can learn from the other. No one has a monopoly on knowledge.

To be flexible is to be able to adjust to various situations and different Personalities with ease. Bending the sapling while it is young is an old phrase which was applied to the rearing of children. Children are like young plants needing the proper environment for growth, productivity and beautification. They must be nourished properly, cuddled up, propped up, buckled up, brushed up, hushed up and written up. Like precious metal, children are more highly appreciated after refinement. I commend you godly mothers along with fathers for bringing out the best in your children.

In the area of being responsible, Timothy, even though young, could handle responsibility. How much can our children handle? Have they been properly trained? Are we well equipped? Are children getting too many material things that they lose sight on goals, achievements and values? Is there a concern for immediate pleasure rather than a long term benefit? How much input has there been in studying God's word with the children? Parents should not hand their Children over body, mind and soul to the educational system, physicians, psychologists, psychiatrist or religious sect. I commend parents who will not compromise their positions on right but will make their homes the center of Christian training, the center of Christian light, discipline and love.

Having reached almost as far as he could, Paul, an aged man in prison, abandoned by most of his friends is reaching out for Timothy charging him to be strong in the faith; knowledgeable and on guard against those who depart from the Truth of the Gospel, desiring to lead others astray. In reaching others for Christ a new family relationship is created. In Matthew 12:50 Jesus said, *"For whosoever shall do the will of my Father, who is in heaven, the same is my brother, and sister, and mother."* Thank God for the new relationship and the extended family. One cannot under estimate the value of extended families of mothers; foster mothers, adopted mothers, godmothers and Christian mothers. Their love, instructions, influence have proven to be powerful upon lives and our society. Those who bring sunshine into the lives of others cannot keep it from themselves.

Many of you are to be commended for having added joy to my life as members of the extended family. Two younger mothers (far younger than myself) made an indelible imprint upon my life one year when they left their own families behind and traveled hundreds of miles to be with me on a special occasion and presented me with roses. What a sacrifice! You are indeed my children in the Lord. May our relationship grow stronger and more meaningful.

Now I would like to recall the beautiful memories of my own mother who departed this life years ago leaving a rich inheritance of godly instructions and examples to the children and family.

There were many experiences of joys and sorrows, sickness and health, praying and counseling, sharing and withholding, praising and rebuking, behaving and misbehaving, forgiving and forgetting, an outburst of affection on the part of one and a spirit of jealousy by the other.

The conclusion of the whole matter is that genuine love must become the dominating factor in our lives. Those lovable, teachable, flexible and responsible qualities will out-live time and space.

MY CHRISTIAN MOTHER

Barbara Walton

Through your loving and gentle heart, I have learned more about trusting and sharing. Through all of the thoughtfulness you show to everyone you know, I have learned more about loving and caring. Somehow, I say the least to those I love the best; so Christian Mother, let me take a little time to tell you the rest.

Thanks for all your thoughtfulness, your understanding too. Thanks for all the nice things you so generously do. Thanks for the good example you have always set. Thanks for being the best Christian Mother yet. You are wonderful in all the ways that count; giving help and good advice in just the right amount. You might not admit it but you are a warm and loving Christian Mother, considerate and kind. You are someone I feel fortunate to have always on my mind.

THE BASIC FOUR R'S OF REACHING TEENS

It is horrendous that in this enlightened age we are creating a generation of immoral, permissive, rebellious, disrespectful, distorted-minded individuals. The myriad undesirable exposures through electronic equipment, entertainment and the media have been devastating. Crimes and criminals are increasing at an alarming rate. Silence the Violence, Fill the Churches Instead of the Jails, Say No to Dope and numerous other slogans are ineffective. Having witnessed gross neglect and departure from traditional moral values, where do we go from here? Who is to blame? Where do we start for the restoration of law and order in our bizarre society?

Recognition should be our first step: Recognizing Needs that extend beyond the basic elements of food, raiment and shelter. The home is the preparation ground for life activities and development. Be it ever so humble or super affluent, the seed of righteousness must be planted. Each child is a distinct personality and is in need of love, discipline, education and preparation to become a functional mature adult in this competitive society. Acts of aggression, distraction or violence may just be cues for deeper concerns – a problem lurking in disguise. Flowers are nurtured, vegetable gardens cultivated, animals groomed and domesticated; yet, it seems that children are left out in the cold to develop on their own.

Secondly, Reverence for God is paramount in the life of an individual if there is to be any significant regard for the rights of others. Placing reverence second does not negate the fact that God is first in our lives. The first commandment is, *"Thou shalt have no other gods before me."* In essence there must be a reminder of who God is to set the stage for action. In Deuteronomy 5, Moses called the people to attention by saying, *"Hear, O Israel."* In other words, stop, listen and consider who God is and what He has done for you; hear of Him and press forward in obedience to His Word and Will.

Getting the attention of teens and reminding them of the ever-present powerful God who controls the universe are basics. Nevertheless, living a godly life and setting concrete examples speak louder than words. There is more adult delinquency than juvenile. Teens see the pattern of flakiness and hypocrisy demonstrated by professing adult Christians and are turned off.

Thirdly, <u>Respect</u> for All People. People are human, different in color, creed, nationality and personality; endowed by the Creator with certain inherent rights that should be preserved and respected. Defining where one's rights end and the other person's begin is paving the way for a more gentle civilized society. The principle laid down by the Golden Rule is scriptural and applies to elders as well as peers. Elderly citizens are often considered over the hill, less intelligent, disadvantaged, replaceable and unserviceable. Contrary to these opinions, they are the ones who laid the foundation for today's realities through contributions in every area of life. Their fortitude can never be excelled. <u>Obsolete thinking</u> on the part of either; placing the young in the future and the seniors in the distant past is unwise and demeaning. This could easily generate divisiveness and a generation gap; eroding our society and depriving each other of a wonderful caring, sharing relationship and fellowship. Whenever possible, the mature experienced adult should be used to assist in teaching and training the young and then move over to a more comfortable relaxing area, still bringing forth fruit in old age. The area of discipleship as stated in the Great Commission is never crowded.

Fourthly, the sense of <u>Responsibility</u> rests unequivocally with the parents or guardians in the home. If young people are not taught properly and disciplined, they become public liabilities. Deuteronomy 6:6-8 is a reminder to teach, teach, teach diligently! Much emphasis should be placed on the fifth commandment: *Honor thy father and thy mother; that thy days may be long upon the land, which the Lord thy God giveth thee.* Supportive scripture in Ephesians 6 says, *"Children obey your <u>parents in the Lord</u> for this is* *right and ye fathers provoke not your children to wrath: but bring them up in the nurture and admonition of the Lord."* Here we have mutual respect for both parents and children.

Parents are to assist in all developmental processes and provide for adequate secular education. Lead them to accept Christ as Savior at an early age, also become involved in Sunday School and Church activities. Remember to teach them to work with their hands as well as their minds. This is a God-given responsibility.

To reach teens in a meaningful manner, one should be prayerful, loving, kind and thoughtful. Recognition of their needs and meeting the same should be done in spite of personality and manner of dress. Respect the ability to be different but not radical. There must be a reminder, however, that some bizarre hair styles and dress may deprive one of employment in the business or professional society. Become a part of their Christian involvement as well as the secular. The Bible has the answers for reaching teens. The responsibility belongs to you, the parent, as well as to you, the adult.

USING TIME WISELY

Ephesians 5:15-21

Bitterness, resentment, or retaliation had no place in the life of Paul. This letter to the Ephesians was written during his first imprisonment in Rome; nevertheless, he did not permit this physical restraint to disturb his inner peace or spiritual zeal. He continued to exhort the saints to live a life consistent with the principles laid down by our Lord and Savior Jesus Christ.

Righteous living and wise use of time have always been God's plan and will for man. Those who use time wisely have been rewarded, whereas, those who squandered time have suffered loss or have had many, many regrets.

Paul was well qualified to exhort the saints to use time wisely his was the voice of experience. You may recall how he wasted the church while riding high in Judaism, following the tradition of men; flaunting a busy mind but going in the wrong direction. God in due time knocked him down, picked him up, cleansed him mentally and spiritually, transformed his life to the extent he knew what it meant to walk circumspectly.

King Solomon, in all his wisdom and earthly glory, squandered much time attempting to satisfy his own ego and passion. He searched vainly to gain deeper insight into the unknown only to discover late in life that all was vanity and vexation of spirit. However, he left on record many words of wisdom in Proverbs and Ecclesiastes summing up the whole matter of living successfully. *"Fear God and keep His commandments for this is the whole duty of man."*

Webster's dictionary sets forth twenty definitions for the noun time making it one of the longest definitions in the book. Since I cannot explain or retain many of them, please permit me to use a personal concept to coincide with the theme.

Time is a priceless gift from God which He entrust to every person for a season. He alone gives, sustains and retrieves it. Time cannot be bought, sold, traded or exchanged; just a golden opportunity and ever-present resource. One minute is all we have at one time sixty seconds in it; if you don't use it, you lose it and can never retrieve it. We can all attest to the fact that one moment we may be enjoying life and another moment hurled into eternity. <u>Now</u> is the appointed time.

Begin in the home using time wisely. Like Mary of Bethany, sit at the feet of Jesus and be blessed. Train up a child in the way he should go. Spend more time in <u>prayer</u> and setting examples. Examples speak louder than words. Establish excellent communication and disciplinary methods as a matter of correction and effective teaching. Proper grooming is never outdated. Do not contribute to the evil times.

Parents should be involved in the schools, in the educational and recreational activities of their children. Take time out to instill in them respect for elders, their peers and educators. Spend time wisely in assisting children to set forth realistic goals for the future and encourage them to achieve. When rewards or recognition are given for achievements, they should not be considered a <u>payoff</u> policy.

In the Church, more time should be spent in family worship, worshipping in tithes and offering, studying together, demonstrating love, compassion for all people especially the less fortunate. Find real joy in the Lord so that wherever you go there is a song ringing in your heart.

Community time - become involved in community activities. Prepare children to live productively and with some potentials for being good citizens, giving to society instead of seeking to receive. Send children out with something in their hands and heads. The lad with the lunch that was used by Jesus to feed the multitude is a marvelous example of a child in the right place at the right time with the right attitude and right something for the right person. Remember now thy Creator in the days of thy youth, while the evil days come not, nor the years draw night when thou shalt say, I have no pleasure in them.

Missionaries, it is time to be wise, time to be sober; time to organize and utilize time to the glory of God and benefit of mankind. Time to share the Good News of salvation. Time to understand that the last letter in time is the first letter in eternity. Time to know that if you reverse the letter in time you have the word e-m-i-t. If time is not used wisely, you may be emitting extremely toxic chemicals in a heavily polluted evil society. God forbids!

Time to live so not to contribute to evil days. Time to refrain from divisions in homes and churches, in order that you may have a vision of Christ - high and lifted up. Time to build walls of service and fellowship. Time to be a voice in the wilderness, a city that sets on a hill and time to be salt that will help to season the world.

GOD'S MIRACULOUS SAVING POWER IN 1987 CHILDREN: A LIVING TESTIMONY

Cecelia Shihan was a lone survivor of flight 225 in Michigan, August 16, 1987, where more than one hundred others perished, including her parents. Jessica McClure was rescued from an abandoned deep well through God's power and the untiring efforts of diligent workers.

Baby Doe survived a devastating earthquake in Mexico after having been buried alive under debris for days.

Baby X survived a raging tornado in Memphis, Arkansas on December 14th. Many others lost their lives and property.

Recognizing the inability of these young survivors to remember the dates or catastrophic conditions, history stands as a reminder of God's omnipotent power where He did not leave Himself without a witness. He still speaks through disaster as well as through the stillness of nature but always through the Written Word, the Holy Bible and Living Word, Jesus Christ. God is always in control of the universe. We, as well as these children, are witnesses of His Saving Grace.

MY HERO

My hero is God. He wakes me up every morning and starts me on my way. He is real to me. He will always be in my heart. You can also feel Him in your heart.

He died on the cross for you and me. He's my all and all.

In Acts 14:17, it says that God gives us "fruitful seasons," and for this, I give thanks unto the Lord. God is my Holy Ghost.

Cassandra MacGregor
Thirkell School, Age 10

HAVE YOU LOST SOMEONE?

Have you lost the Living Word? The Living Word is Jesus Christ, our Savior. St. John 1:1, *"In the beginning was the Word and the Word was with God and the Word was God."* St. John 1:14, *"And the Word was made flesh, and dwelt among us, (and we beheld his glory, the glory as of the only begotten of the Father), full of grace and truth."*

If you have ever lost a relative, close friend or even had someone missing in action, I am sure you know the awesome feeling of broken relationship, heart rending grief, unfulfilled dreams and loneliness. There is a void that cannot be filled and a hunger for reconciliation.

Mary and Joseph, the parents of Jesus, lost Him at the age of twelve in the temple at Jerusalem. They traveled a day's journey toward home without recognizing his absence; supposing He was traveling with relatives and acquaintances? After three days they found Him and were reconciled.

Can you think of any instance in which you have left Christ behind? Do you take Him to school, work or to your social and political events? Is He your business partner? Do you get preoccupied with family and friends leaving Him behind? Have you lost the joy of His salvation? Are you cold, calculating and indifferent toward others? Let Him be you constant companion and you will experience unspeakable joy.

Seek Him while He may be found. Say as the disciples did when Christ revealed Himself to them, *"Abide with us: for it is toward evening and the day is far spent."* He went in, tarried with them and their eyes were opened to His presence. Let Him open your eyes so that you may behold wonderful things out of the Word, and be marvelously blessed!

HAVE YOU LOST A BIBLE?

The Bible is the Written Word given by inspiration to holy men of old. All scripture is given by inspiration of God, and is profitable for doctrine, for reproof, for correction, for instruction in righteousness - 2 Timothy 3:16.

While many newspapers and periodicals have lost and found columns, I cannot recall any advertisement concerning a Bible being lost, found or reward offered. Most Bibles are lost in homes and in Churches. They are lost literally because of willful neglect to study; physically because of sentimental values; without concern for the substance; spiritually by failure to hide its words in your heart so that you may not sin against God. Have you lost a Bible?

When the temple was being repaired during the reign of king Josiah (2 Chronicles 34), the book of the law was found by Hilkiah, the priest. The book had been lost for many years. When it was read before the king, he was exceedingly sorry because they had not kept the law leaving them vulnerable for divine judgment.

What is you reaction to the Written Word? Have you lost it? Treasured it? Meditated upon it? Have you applied it to your daily living, making it the most utilized book in the home? Now is the time for all people, especially Christians to make the Bible relevant in their lives. Read it to be wise, study it to be knowledgeable and obey it to be changed. In wisdom, someone has said so well, that the Bible never suffers neglect; it is only those who neglect it who suffer.

THE BODY OF CHRIST
(THE FEET)

I will praise the Lord; for I am fearfully and wonderfully made. Marvelous are thy works; and that my soul knoweth right well.
Psalm 139:14

God, the Father, Creator and Sustainer of life has fashioned man in a magnificent manner, unique in physical being, endowed with a spiritual nature that grows only as it communicates and reaches upward to God. In Him we live, move and have our being, therefore, we should magnify His name for He is worthy.

Feet are important members of our bodies. They are the terminal portion of the body; consisting of many bones; long, short, rounded and flat; joining together with the structure of the legs to function in various ways. Examples: Supporting the structure, walking, standing, running and relaxing.

The feet support the entire structure of the body, whether large or small, young or old, curved, flat or straight. As I think of feet, they remind me of faith--the foundation of our Christian life. Not just the end but the beginning of our movements in all directions. We can do all things through Christ who strengthens us.

<u>Walking feet:</u> *"Blessed is the man that walketh not in the counsel of the ungodly."* Psalm 1:1. *"How beautiful upon the mountain are the feet of him that bringeth good tidings that publisheth peace."* Isaiah 52:7a.

How important it is that we use our feet to walk in the path of righteousness, to spread the good news of our Savior and become a peaceful walker in this confused world. There is therefore no condemnation of them who are in Christ, who walk not after the flesh, but the spirit - Romans 8:1-4.

<u>Standing feet</u>: *"I was glad when they said unto me: let us go into the house of the Lord; our feet shall stand within thy gates, O Jerusalem."* Psalm 122:1-2

Stand, therefore, steadfast in the faith for he who does not stand for what is right will fall for anything.

<u>Running feet</u>: *"Know ye not that they who run in a race, run all, but one receiveth the prize? So run, that ye may obtain."* 1 Corinthians 9:24

"But they that wait upon the Lord shall renew their strength; they shall mount up with wings like eagles; they shall run and not be weary and they shall walk and not faint." Isaiah 40:31

<u>Leaping feet</u>: *"Rejoice ye in that day and leap for joy; for behold your reward is great in heaven."* Luke 6:23

<u>Guiding feet</u>: *"Thy word is a lamp unto my feet and a light unto my path."* Psalm 119:105

There are also humble feet, anointed feet, clean feet and blessed feet. When we use our feet and all the energy supplied through them, we can truly rest in the Lord knowing that He who has begun a good work in us will complete it to the end. We can finally say I have fought a good fight. I have finished my course. I have kept the faith.

THE HAND OF GOD

This publication is a living testimony to the power of God in my life--blessing, healing, shaping and permitting me to share with others.

Many years ago, I suffered excruciating pain in both eyes as a result of infection. I questioned the prognosis as to whether I would sustain permanent visual damage. My immediate attitude became that of racing with time; doing things in a positive but expeditious manner before tragedy strikes. Prayers, meditations on God's goodness and faith sustained me through those months of suffering and healing. Six weeks passed before the infection responded to professional treatment. Finally I concluded that God had used this method to test my faith; as a time element to teach me patience, to invigorate my mind and to enrich me spiritually with much of what is delivered in this book.

Truly I can testify that the hand of God is Omnipotent. *"All power is given unto me in heaven and in earth."*

His hand is an intervening hand.
Wait on the Lord.

His hand is an anointing hand.
He healeth all of our diseases.

His hand is a providing hand.
I shall not want.

His hand is a protecting hand.
Except the Lord build the house, they labor in vain that build it.

His hand is a comforting hand.
Thy rod and thy staff they comfort me.

His hand is an uplifting hand.
Love lifted me.

His hand is a strengthening hand
I can do all things through Christ which strengtheneth me.

His hand is a directing hand.
He shall direct thy paths.

His hand is a caring hand.
He careth for you.

His hand is a blessing hand.
The Lord bless thee and keep thee.

His hand is a consecrated hand.
Consecrate me Lord to thy service.

His hand is a preserving hand.
Preserve me, O God: for in thee I put my trust.

His hand is a saving hand.
Behold the Lord's hand is not shortened that He cannot save.

His hand is an eternal hand
"And I give unto them eternal life;
and they shall never perish, neither shall any man pluck them
out of My Father's hand."

Anonymous

PATIENCE

J. D. Douglas' Bible Dictionary states that Biblical patience is a God-exercised, or God-given restraint in face of opposition or oppression. Therefore having experienced certain difficulties and illness I can agree with many others that Christian patience is of God. It is not a forced situation or condition in which one may find himself unwilling to reveal his true nature or force a smile rather than frown; leaving himself with a deep seated emotional problem and sometime a self inflicted headache.

Patience is not just sitting idly by waiting for progress or resigned to circumstances. It is actively engaging in what-ever there is to be done to the glory of God. One must work with all one's might as if everything depended on the individual's effort, praying and waiting for the result; knowing full well that everything depends on God.

The Old Testament from Genesis to Malachi shows God's patience in dealing with sinfulness, His promise of a Savior; His protecting mark on Cain, the murderer; His providential rainbow in the sky and His restoration of disobedient Israel. In the New Testament and throughout the church age God is continually pleading and bearing with the saved and unsaved. He is deferring the second corning of Christ because He is not willing that any should perish but that all should come to repentance.

Remarkable patience was shown in the life of Job. During his suffering friends turned against him; accused him of being unfaithful to God; his wife asked that he curse God and die. Yet he was patience in his endurance and remained true to God. Who can measure up to this?

Jesus Christ the Supreme Example was oppressed, afflicted, brought as a lamb to the slaughter and as a sheep before her shearer, is dumb so He opened not His mouth (Isaiah 53:7). He has set the example. Are we willing to follow?

The word patience is written more than forty four times in the Holy Bible. In the Epistle of James to the twelve tribes because of persecution, we find the word patience five times, patient two times and references to endurance and testing of faith throughout the five Chapters.

Exercises in patience may be bitter but the fruits are plentiful and sweet. You may gain inner strength, inspiration, courage, defuse a time bomb and increase in your personal relationship with God and man.

In a craft section of a department store I once observed a knitted object with dangling threads indicating it was just short of being completed. Upon close observation I read, "Be careful, my maker in not yet finished with me."

In as much as God is still working with us and in us to perfect our patience, let us exemplify it in our lives.

LONGSUFFERING

From the theme we shall focus on three factors; (1) The longsuffering of God for wayward man, (2) the longsuffering of Jesus for humanity and (3) the lack of suffering on the part of believers today.

First factor. Does God really suffer? If so, how long is His suffering? God does suffer in that He is slow to anger which is an extension of mercy and patience. He is longsuffering to us, not willing that any should perish, but that all should come to repentance (2 Peter 3:9). God's suffering is eternal. *"Yea, I have loved thee with an everlasting love therefore with loving kindness have I drawn thee"* (Jeremiah 31:3). Have you recognized the drawing power of God?

Eight souls were saved from the flood because of God's extended longsuffering. This was not due to their righteousness, but because of one man--Noah, who found grace in the sight of God.

Through eight covenants, forty two generations and four hundred years of silence when there was no inspirational message from God to man, His longsuffering prevailed. What was God doing? Delaying justice and preparing a human sacrificial Lamb, His Only Begotten Son for the salvation of mankind,

Second factor. Finally Jesus Christ came on the scene, fulfilled the promises of the Old Testament and established the New Covenant. Isaiah 53 tells of His suffering, He suffered through misunderstandings of family, friends, disciples also enemies; was finally denied, forsaken and crucified. Thank God for His victory over death through His resurrection and ascension!

Third factor. If you were to take a retrospective view of the longsuffering of God and the continuation of the same in Jesus Christ, in what light would you find yourself: standing, kneeling, bowing or falling prostrate at the feet of the Savior pleading for unmerited favors? Ask yourself the following questions. How deserving am I of His loving kindness? Am I really tolerant of my fellowman? Do I love in the spirit of Christianity? Am I suffering long for lost souls or am I satisfied that Christ has made me whole? Why not probe your own heart, soul and mind; feel your own spiritual pulse; take your own religious blood pressure and accept the therapy of the Holy Spirit.

I challenge you today to recognize where you stand in the light of God's suffering and resolve to extend to your fellowman similar consideration. In return you will receive the blessedness of a richer fuller peaceful life.

CLOTHINGS

Clothing is an integral part of our society. They are worn for coverings, protection, respectability, beautification, entertainment and recreation. The first use was by our fore-parents, Adam and Eve, after their sinful act of disobedience in the Garden of Eden. The sewing together of fig leaves to hide their nakedness and humiliation was at the least inadequate, flimsy and perishable. God, as Creator and Sustainer of the universe, gave them a more durable protection, the covering of animal skins.

We are reminded that without the shedding of blood there is no protection, no salvation, no remission of sin. Jesus Christ covered our sins on Calvary, nailed our selfishness to the cross of forgiveness, crossed out our debts and paid the price by death for our waywardness.

Let us not be weary or exalted in well-doing. Many have lost their moral standing and others their lives lusting after fashionable expensive garments and ornaments.

Sometime ago, I heard a pastor's remarked that years ago it took much cotton to make a skirt for a woman, but today they are so microscopic that an insect could easily weave one. His analogy was one of distaste and distraction.

Since appropriate clothing is available for every occasion, no committed Christian should have problems presenting him or herself for worship before the King of kings in a sacred, serious, spiritual manner.

The Lord looks at the heart and judges the same accordingly, while man looks on the exterior. *"Wherefore, if meat makes my brother to offend, I will eat no flesh while the world standeth, lest I make my brother to offend"* (1 Corinthians 8:13).

It is a blessing to be able to dress proudly, gracefully, sensibly and becomingly for every occasion. Come now and let us worship together in spirit and in truth. *"God is a Spirit: and they that worship Him must worship Him in spirit and in Truth"* (St. John 4:24).

CHRISTIAN DRESS CODE

How well do we know that too much emphasis is placed on outward appearance as opposed to inward righteousness? The adorning of the saints should be manifested in the intrinsic beauty of a meek and gentle spirit, which is precious in the sight of God. I Peter 3:3-4.

In Isaiah's prophesy concerning the forthcoming judgment of Judah, he warned of severe punishment upon the women for their haughtiness, vain display of ornaments and rich apparel (Isaiah 3:16-24).

Don't copy the behavior and customs of this world, but be a new and different person with a fresh newness in all you do and think. Then you will learn from your own experience how His ways will really satisfy you (Romans 12:2, The Living Bible).

AUTUMN

Autumn is the season of the year between summer and winter beginning somewhere between the third week in September and ending somewhere near the third week in December. It is a time of quiet activity generally, referred to as the fall of the year. Having heard and visualized all of the joys of spring and the splendor of summer, I am sure you would like to fall away from all the excitement and relax in the haze of Autumn.

The first letter is A: one of <u>activities</u>: Proverbs 3:1-2. A time of harvesting, gathering of crops and storing away for the anticipated unfavorable wintry days. In the process of canning, it must be remembered that we must not can all we can and then sit on the can. It is a time of sharing cans.

The second activity of A is <u>aging</u>. It is not surprising to awaken some morning in September or October to find a variety of colors; green, yellow, gold, brown and a deepened hue of red that can never be duplicated. This is the work of the Creator over His Creation; the process of natural decay. They have finished their offering of service to God and man. From this we learn to do our work well in the prime of life in due season and be ready to depart when called (John 12:24).

U - <u>Understanding.</u> Proverbs 3:13 *Happy is the man that findeth wisdom and the man that getteth understanding.* As we understand what is happening in the natural realm of time, we should be capable of making them a reality in our lives.

T - Teaching, training, traditions, turkeys and Thanksgiving. These are times of greater involvements; children being taught at home and school is essential for a meaningful well balanced fruitful life. The family tradition of togetherness, fun, food, events shared during Thanksgiving season is exciting and memorable.

U - Unyielding. Autumn is that time in an individual's life that he may be classified as over the hill, mature and mellow. Experience should have taught many lessons of strong personality, unyielding to the winds of temptation; standing in the face of disastrous and serene when the first snow falls. Be able to do all things through Christ who strengthens you (Philippians 4:13).

M - Meditation. Time for reflection; thinking on the goodness of God who has sustained, protected and empowered us through the years and still working mightily in our lives.

N - Nurture. The Psalmist, David feasted on the Word of God. O taste and see that the Lord is good; blessed is the man that trusteth in Him (Psalm 34:8).

To enjoy the blessings and essence of autumn one must be truly committed to God's Word. One's mind must be centered on things that are lovely, pure, honest, just, and of good report. One can delight himself or herself in the colors of autumn. The green - enrichment to life; brown - maturity and mellowness of life; yellow - caution; red hue - still some excitement left. One can't help being excited about the saving blood of Jesus Christ. Gold - the serenity of grace. White - cleansing and purity. Autumn is truly a time of sharing: sharing our hopes, our dreams our substances, our faith in God, in our fellowman and our country for a better tomorrow.

Histories

HISTORY OF FATHER'S DAY

This is a very Special Day set aside by our National Government to honor fathers. However, the original day was designated by God in the Ten Commandments. *"Honor thy father and thy mother"* is the first commandment with promise.

How appropriate it is to express gratitude and appreciation in unforgettable ways to those who labored faithfully to support, protect and encourage their families. Fathers often remain in the background, but their love and influence have a profound impact upon their children.

Mrs. John Bruce Dodd of Spokane, Washington, started Father's Day in 1910. Later the custom spread throughout the United States. In 1936, a National Father's Day committee was formed with headquarters in New York City. Father's Day is observed the third Sunday in June. The Father of the year is elected annually. Among men chosen have been Douglas MacArthur, Ralph J. Bunch, Dwight D. Eisenhower and Harry S. Truman.

Fathers are to remember someone is watching to follow in their footsteps. Don't forget to wear appropriate shoes so that those following will not become misfits.

HISTORY OF MOTHER'S DAY

The observance of Mother's Day began in the old world with the most noted documentation in England. However, its roots are in the Ten Commandments found in Exodus 20:12. "Honor thy father and thy mother, that the days may be long upon the land which the Lord thy God giveth thee." Julia Ward Howe made the first known suggestion for a Mother's Day in U.S.A. in 1872. She suggested that people observe a Mother's Day on June 2nd, a day dedicated to peace. For several years, she held an annual Mother's Day in Boston. Following this, others launched campaigns for Mother's Day.

Anna Javis of Philadelphia launched a nationwide observance for Mother's Day in 1907. When she was asked by the superintendent of the Sunday School in a Virginia town, in which her deceased mother had long been the moving spirit, to arrange a memorial, she consented gladly and the impact was profound upon communities. She chose the 2nd Sunday in May and began the custom of wearing a carnation. This flower is one which the petals never fall, but merely wither symbolic of mother's ever-abiding love.

A resolution from delegates at a general conference of the Methodist Episcopal Church was introduced to recognize Anna Javis as the founder of Mother's Day.

A proclamation by President Woodrow Wilson, also by a Joint Resolution approved May 8, 1914, designating the second Sunday in May as Mother's Day.

THE HISTORY OF CHILDREN'S DAY

The observance of the second Sunday in June as Children's Day by the Protestant churches began in the middle of the last century. The earliest observance of which any record has been found was arranged by the Rev. Dr. Charles H. Leonard, pastor of the Universalist Church of the Redeemer in Chelsa, Massachusetts. It was on the second Sunday in June, 1856, when a special service was held for the children and when those who had not been baptized were Christened. Dr. Leonard called the day Rose Sunday. The day was later called Flower Sunday, but in the course of a few years it came to be known as Children's Day.

The Methodist Episcopal Church was the first denomination formally to recognize the day. Its adoption was recommended in 1865, and in 1866 the general conference voted that the second Sunday in June be observed in honor of the children. A children's service was held in Camden, New Jersey on that day in 1866, and in 1867 the general convention of the Universalist Church recommended that this day be adopted as the time for the baptism of children.

Like many American customs, the observance of Children's Day has its roots in the old world. May Day was the day on which children were confirmed in the Roman and the Lutheran Churches. The children carried flowers in a procession to the churches. The change from May Day to June is a natural shifting of the date to conform with the season of flowers, especially in the northern part of the country.

EASTER

In Christian lands the greatest religious festival of the year is Easter. It takes place on the first Sunday following the full moon that appears on or after the vernal equinox (the day in the spring when the sun crosses the equator and the day and night are of equal length), about March 21. It is preceded by the six weeks following Ash Wednesday, a period of fasting set aside for mourning the trial and crucifixion of Christ. The churches are usually filled to overflowing with people dressed in new Easter costumes; the altar is banked with lilies and spring flowers; and the choir and congregation join in singing joyous hymns and anthems.

Easter is also a springtime festival, and many customs are pagan in origin, having nothing to do with Christianity. The name Easter comes from the Scandinavian "Ostra" and the Teutonic "Ostern," both goddesses of mythology signifying the coming of spring. This celebration is closely tied to nature worship; for instance, the symbolic use of eggs and the Easter hare both have a mystical background. Even the ancients knew that all elemental matter is oval-shaped, from the rain drop to the seed; therefore, the Easter egg pays tribute to life outgrowth of the ancient pagan sacramental cakes eaten by Anglo-Saxons in honor of their goddess. The cross is a symbol of many creeds.

In the Orient, the Easter hare (bunny) is very closely associated with the new moon. The Europeans also have all sorts of fantasies connected with the moon, but the most accepted theory is that it represents fertility.

It was a common belief among the early Christians that on Easter morning the sun danced in honor of the resurrection and people rose long before the sun to see the feat. We should rise early to see the beauty of each day and walk in the newness of life.

THANKSGIVING
A Harvest Festival

Harvest Festival, historically, dates back to God's laws and ordinances for the Israelites in Exodus 23:16 and Exodus 34:22. Following many years of social economics and cultural transitions, what was originally called the Feast of Harvest emerged into picturesque parades of happy people bearing the first fruit or grain through the streets in honor of the gods who foster crops. Out of these observances, our present Thanksgiving Day came into existence.

Harvest Festivals, traditionally, were not only a scene of merriment and hospitality but a time for temporary suspension of equality between master and servant. Following the gathering of crops, it was natural then for the people to laugh and sing when their barns were full and work in the hot summer was over. This became a wonderful time to express joy and give thanks for something that had happened.

It was autumn of 1621, in Plymouth Colony, when Governor Bradford followed the custom that had been observed in one way or another for many centuries, set a time for giving thanks for the year's harvest. He also decided to make it an occasion for strengthening friendship with the Indians; so, an invitation was sent to Chief Massaasiot and his braves to share in the festival. They were pleased to accept and sent five deer as a gift for the feast.

The people at Plymouth, Massachusetts, reenact the first American Thanksgiving each year. Dressed in colonial costumes, they gather at the famous rock and bow their heads in gratitude.

Thanksgiving dinners are family affairs and celebrated almost entirely within the home. One fine way in which the people celebrate is to attend church service in the morning and in many localities, persons of different denominations worship together. It is a time of sharing with the less fortunate. Churches, schools and various societies see to it that no one goes hungry.

Thanksgiving Day in the United States of America, a national holiday, usually the fourth Thursday of November is set aside annually for thanksgiving and praises to God.

Book of Festival Holidays
Marguerite Ickis

HISTORY OF WOMAN'S DAY
The Idea, Purpose and Plan

The Idea, Purpose and Plan of WOMAN'S DAY was first presented by Nannie H. Burroughs, the young Corresponding Secretary of the Woman's Convention, Auxiliary to the National Baptist Convention, in her report at the meeting of the Convention, in Memphis, Tennessee, September, 1906.

The work of the Woman's Convention had hardly begun. At that time, Nannie Burroughs was being dubbed an "upstart", and to this unkind thrust she was provoked to answer back, "I might be an 'upstart', but I am also starting up." The new Convention voted to accept the Woman's day suggestion of its Corresponding Secretary.

Her proposal as to time was that the fourth Sunday in July be known as National WOMAN'S DAY. Why July?

WOMAN'S DAY was set for late July, because by that time most State Convention activities have ended for the year, and workers in local churches--under less strain--would be able to give full time and attention to learning speeches and soliciting gifts, preparatory to the "Great Day."

The purpose of the day was to interest women of the local churches in raising money for Foreign Missions. This National day was proposed because the chief interest of the Woman's Convention, at its beginning, was to raise money for Foreign Missions. The Woman's Convention then had its office in the Headquarters of the Foreign Mission Board at Louisville, Kentucky.

The Corresponding Secretary suggested that in order to interest and develop the women, that the Secretary be permitted to prepare and send out the program and three special addresses (short but challenging) on Missions or on some kindred phase of that subject and that the speeches by written from research and study of firsthand current information about the Missionary enterprise. It was pointed out that the material for the addresses furnished would be committed to memory by speakers selected by the Missionary Society and thus the Convention could discover and develop public speak- ers for church programs, particularly for Woman's Day. This day was not thought up as a scheme for raising money, but primarily for <u>raising women.</u>

Because of the way the purpose of WOMAN'S DAY has been diverted, our churches are reaping a financial harvest for church buildings, improvements and every conceivable local benefit. The promoters send off each year to get a WOMAN'S DAY speaker; somebody who can draw a crowd. Had the original plan been followed, the churches would now have well-prepared speakers of their own. WOMAN'S DAY would be a real educational and spiritual achievement, blessing the local churches beyond imagination. Many women thus discovered and given opportunity to develop would be "tops" in Christian service. People would pack the church to see and hear their own discovery.

The day offers a glorious opportunity for women to learn to speak for themselves and thus become sublime symbols of devotions, lofty ideals, courage, fidelity and grace.

Gems of purest ray serene are in our churches.

"WOMAN'S DAY," properly used, would put women's feet in the path of service and lift their heads up to see the field ripe unto harvest. But instead, women prance up and down church aisles, passing envelopes and baskets begging for money to beat the men.

WOMAN'S DAY should mean Woman's Supreme Opportunity to do what the woman did who talked with Jesus at the well. That woman "went to town" and brought the town out to "see Jesus."

Nannie H. Burroughs,
Excerpts from 1968 Nannie H. Burroughs Publications

CONTRIBUTIONS: PEOPLE OF COLOR IN BIBLE HISTORY

God, out of one blood, made all the nations of the world. However, He prepared, chose and called out of slavery the Jews (Hebrews or Israelites) to become a nation through which the Savior would come and all <u>nations</u> would be blessed. Contributions have been made by all nations. Nevertheless, Africa and Egypt have had remarkable and tremendous influence upon the religious and cultural development of the Old and New Testaments, which are scarcely recognized.

All biblical nations descended from Noah's three sons. From Shem came the Hebrews, Chaldeans, Persians and Syrians. Japheth's descendants are Greeks, Thracians and Scythians. Ham's descendants are Canaanites, Egyptians, Philistines, Hittites, Amorites, Jebusites and Assyrians (see Life Application Bible Exposition KJV, page 23 and Genesis, Chapter Ten). Ham's descendants settled in Canaan, Egypt and the surrounding region of Africa.

Nimrod, son of Cush, Ham's grandson and Noah's great grandson, a hunter, warrior and king, was the first great builder recorded in biblical history. Genesis 10:10. The beginning of his kingdom was Babel, and Erech and Accad and Cabreh, in the land of Shinar (Babylon).

"Out of that land went Asshur and builded Nineveh, and the city Rehoboth and Calah" Genesis 10:11.

Mizraim, second son of Ham, has been recorded by secular history as the ancestor founder of the Egyptians. In the Old Testament, the nation of Egypt is sometimes called Mizraim.

Moses belonged to the tribe of Levi of the family of Amram but grew up in the enrichment and <u>wisdom</u> of the Egyptian society He was the great leader and lawgiver through whom God brought the Hebrews out of Egypt. <u>Forty years of preparation took place in Egypt.</u> The name of Moses extends throughout the Old and New

Testaments.

Rahab, the harlot, a Canaanite, became a heroine of Israel who saved the two spies from Jericho's militia by hiding them on the roof of her house. Joshua 6:17; 22-25. She was included in the faith hall of fame, Hebrews 11:31; in James 2:25 as one who was justified by her works and in Matthew 1:5 as an ancestor of Jesus Christ.

Zerah, the Ethiopian king, came out in forceful military strength against King Asa of Judah and his army; subdued them until the king petitioned God for deliverance. His prayer was answered. 2 Chronicles 14:9-15. For many years, Egypt formed an alliance with Ethiopia. Approximately sixty years Ethiopian rules controlled the Nile Valley[1] but were later reduced to tributary status.

Ebed-Melech, Ethiopian servant of Jedekiah, rescued Jeremiah from the dungeon and whose life was spared as a reward (Jeremiah 38:7-13).

Queen of Sheba has been referred to by some scholars as a woman of color. She tested Solomon with hard questions and discovered his wisdom exceeded his fame (1 King 10:1-13). Some scholars believed she represented the region of Ethiopia, south of Egypt, while others insisted she ruled among the tribes of southwestern Arabia. Jesus Christ referred to her as the queen of the south (Matthew 12:42).

The New Testament Church crosses cultural, economical, intellectual and social barriers. Now there were in the church which was at Antioch certain prophets and teachers; as Barnabas, and **Simeon that was called Niger.** and Lucius **of Cyrene**. And when they had fasted and prayed and laid their hands on them, they sent them out (Acts 13:1). (Paul and Barnabas commissioned for the first missionary journey).

---

[1] Wood, D. R. W., Wood, D. R. W., & Marshall, I. H. 1996, c1982, c1962. *New Bible Dictionary.* Includes index. (electronic ed. of 3rd ed.) . InterVarsity Press: Downers Grove

Simon of Cyrene has the distinction of bearing the cross of Jesus to Calvary before his crucifixion.

Alexandra and Rufus the sons of Simon of Cyrene were active in the early church (Mark 15:21 and Romans 16:13).

The first Gentile convert to Christianity was an Ethiopian Eunuch, a high official in the court of Queen Candace. He was converted under Philip's ministry (Acts 8:26-40).

Well known in the Old Testament are Hagar, the Egyptian, and her son Ishmael by Abraham, out of whom God made a great nation.

Yes, Egypt and Africa have given much to civilization. The early childhood of Jesus Christ was spent in Egypt, a flight from Herod who sought to kill him. *"And was there until the death of Herod; that it might be fulfilled which was spoken of the Lord by the prophet, saying, Out of Egypt have I called my son"* (Matthew 2:15).

There were two persons by the name of Cushi, meaning black or Ethiopian, whose contributions cannot be overlooked. One was a messenger of goodwill, an ancestor of Jehudi, whom the Jewish leaders sent to ask Baruch to read the scroll of Jeremiah to them. Jeremiah 36:14

The other Cushi, the son of Gedaliah and the father of the prophet Zephaniah (Zephaniah 1:1). See Nelson Illustrated Bible Dictionary page 2719. Scripturally, we may concede that Zephaniah, the prophet and writer, was the son of an Ethiopian or black man.

In summary all contributions are of divine nature given by inspiration of God so that man may be fully prepared and equipped in every respect to do the will of God (2 Timothy 3:16-17). Thanks be to God that salvation is based upon the sacrificial atonement of Jesus Christ for the sins of the world, which is not about race but all about grace.

HISTORY OF THE WOMEN'S ARMY CORPS

The highway of life is constantly under construction as you well know; women are making remarkable inroads into the main stream. With every entrance and every exit, history is made; with the climbing of each hill and the swerving of each curve, history is made; with the proper decisions at the railroads, crossroads, bridges and inclines, history is made. However, failure to observe the warning signals and speed limits may climax the history-making process.

For many years, females were excluded from enlisting into the military through regulations, legislations and discriminations.

World War II necessitated drastic changes and new avenues were constructed. History was again in the making...with chapters written by women.

During the German conquest in Europe when Hitler had set out to rule the entire world, an idea was conceived by Rep. Edith Norse Roger of Massachusetts. The plan proposed to establish a unit of volunteer women army helpers as temporary skilled workers. They were to receive Medical benefit from the Army while serving but none following discharge, except those provided by the Employees Compensation Commission. In 1941, this bill was introduced to Congress, tossed out and put on hold because of public opinion.

The bill was considered nonsense, demoralizing and unacceptable. The truth of the matter is that any new idea is usually met with suspicion or rejection. The common sense angle is to maintain a wait-and-see attitude. Better still, try it--it just might work. When common sense makes good sense using any other sense is nonsense. Now with so many, negative attitudes and controversies, it became evident that before mobilization was possible public opinion had to be remolded.

Women have always been criticized and stigmatized for adventures beyond the environment of the home or those beyond traditional occupations. How do you offset rumors and public opinions? Frankly, I am not sure but I do know that good examples speak louder than a thousand words. People determine your character by observing what you stand for, what you fall for and what you lie for.

Pearl Harbor was bombed on December 7, 1941: war was declared by President F. D. Roosevelt on December 8. The fighting escalated and in May, 1942, House Resolution 6293 created the WAAC with an authorized strength of 150,000. This Corps paved the way for other branches of the military and was the largest of the Women services in World War II. Recruiting began on May 27, 1942. Who were the recruits? College girls, career women, secretaries, housewives and widows applied. A total of 13,000 was enlisted in one day. On the hot, sticky morning of July 10, 1942, the first volunteers of 440 officers candidates and 330 auxiliaries or privates rolled into Des Moines, Iowa to begin training in the Women's Army Auxiliary Corp.

Just think of women who loved to be different, to bask in their own importance; to wear original frocks and frills; to boast of self-style, individuality in homemaking and social events. They laid aside their personal freedom and sheltered lives for a life of regulations, crude housings, called barracks, and similar uniforms of khaki and olive drab referred to as G.1. (government issue) ill-fitting clothing that was either too large or too small. The shoes were literally boat-like. Alternations within the group solved some of the problems. If you think this was bad, consider the new lingo--mutilated food called "chow," which was so well prepared by army standards that the identity was lost not only to sight but also to taste.

The dining room was called the mess hall. Maybe you can understand why. In spite of this, people looked well and remained healthy.

The lapel emblem worn by the Corp was an image of the Greek goddess of war, Pallas Athena, consisting of a rounded brass button portraying the head of a woman partially covered. This symbolized an appeal to the goddess to assist men during a period of war. The whole thrust behind the auxiliary was to provide skills to release enlisted men for other duties especially combat duties. What were the men's reactions to this? Some reacted with resentment, others with curiosity; but most with deep respect forming a compatible working and friendly relationship. Common sense dictated that it was only a matter of time that kept them from the combat zones.

Women received eight weeks of basic training which were less rigid and less strenuous than their male counterparts. They were treated with respect but not pampered and handled no weapons. Because of physical and psychological differences, women were not put on an equal basis with men, and in my opinion, cannot be.

Following basics, many received specialized training and were sent to various posts throughout the States for duties. They served in more than 235 different army jobs such as; clericals, cooks and bakers, hospital attendants, dental technicians, motor transporters, repairers, communicators and surveyors.

Needless to say, it was summertime but the living was not easy, especially in Des Moines, Iowa. Blacks served under triple discrimination - that of sex, race and military policies. I am sure you are familiar with the old-time way of separate quarters and dining areas, different hours for recreational facilities and of being relegated to minor chores.

Black officers were assigned to command black troops or to serve in administrative capacities. Two exceptions were:

Major Charity Adams, who became supervisor of plans and training at Des Moines and Major Harriett West, who became Chief of Planning Bureau Control Division in Washington. Time, strategies and sit-down strikes eventually alleviated some of the pressures and problems. Through it all, dignity, pride and integrity were maintained by the women. Col. Don C. Faith, Commander of Fort Des Moines and Director Oveta Culp Hobby commended the Corp for supervisor skills and performances.

In September, 1943 the Women Auxiliary Army Corp

(WAAC) was dissolved and replaced by the Women Army Corp (WAC) under which women received full military status in the service. Those desiring to remain in the Army were reunited in Fort Des Moines for a swearing-in ceremony. Others were discharged upon request. Director Hobby was then commissioned Colonel Hobby.

The 688th Central Postal Battalion was the only black WAC unit, assigned to overseas duty, which landed in England, February, 1945 under the command of Major Charity Adams.

Promotions were at a premium and came very slowly. Since the enlisted were replaced by women, it stands to reason that men would receive promotions more readily. The quota system established for the Women's Service Units did not always reward the good or punish the unjust.

Partial desegregation was instituted under the administration of President Harry S. Truman. Even 40 years after World War II, there is much to be desired as we continue our pursuit of life, liberty and happiness.

We pause here to pay tribute to all who served in the Armed Forces of the United States of America. Those who were unable to answer the return roll call are many; we cherish the memories of them with fond devotion. Sgt. Delores Brown, commonly known as "Butch," personally known to me, was a WAC casualty--the result of a Jeep accident. She, too, is numbered with those whose personal sacrifices and patriotism have brought a measurable amount of security to the democratic principles of our country.

Those who survived, we hold in high esteem; their victory testimonies are attributed to Almighty God; yet firmly dedicated to the unfinished task of maintaining a decent live-lihood and peace at home. This is our country, not perfect, but all that we have and we must make it the best to live in.

Those, who fell on the battlefield, their voices are silent; others were weakened due to disability, and still others were silent due to irresponsibility and lack of ambition. True happiness is enjoyed by the wayside and not at the end of the road. Therefore, it behooves all of us to live noble lives, to be responsible citizens; to demand and fight for a wise and honest government assuring equal opportunities, political, social and economic justices for all people. The dignity and future of America and its people depend on jobs--not handouts but workouts. We must be concerned that crime is punished and good conduct commended; we must work fervently for the improvement of human relationships, neighborhoods and communities.

Tributes & Dedications

ODE TO MARTHA

WHO ARE YOU MARTHA?
Grandmother Lula's baby.

MY lovely Aunt is brilliant, tall, statuesque, graceful, soulful, wise, thoughtful, hopeful, gracious, poised, accomplished and so much more.

A woman of Spiritual Depth and the author of several books. You are loving, kind and happy when helping others.

RAISING a standard for others to follow; you lifted the bar up, up and up for each generation to reach for and exceed.

THANK you Lord for filling this angel of a woman with the ability to love, write, organize, teach, lead and mentor.

HELP us to see and to be as God fearing and loving as she. We will reach for the bar to go higher and achieve as much as or more than she.

A Precious Gift to us and to Humanity; you are a woman of worth. You are blessed, successful, respected and honored. Yes, you are Martha, Martha!

By: Margie Lucas

TRIBUTE TO MRS. MARTHA ISHMAEL-BROWN

I am the niece of Mrs. Martha Ishmael Brown the brilliant author of this book. I count it a tremendous honor to be able to write this tribute on behalf of such an inspiring family member that has brought many nuggets of truth and wisdom to bear on our family down through multiple generations. It is so remarkable that Aunt Martha decided to embark upon a third literary endeavor at the young age of 90! We absolutely know "that there is nothing impossible with God" - Luke 1:37.

My Dad was one of Aunt Martha's elder brothers and he always told us children that she was truly "somebody." Aunt Martha was the baby girl of ten siblings and she is the only remaining since the others have all gone on to be with the Lord. To be honest, I didn't realize how smart she was until I enrolled in the same high school that she graduated from. When I arrived there were still a number of her old instructors still teaching at the school who remembered her quite fondly. She was the Salutatorian of her graduating class. Therefore, each one of us who followed in her footsteps, particularly if you carried the last name Ishmael, was expected to live up to the standards that she had set. Despite the weight of that reality - we did A-OK.

Aunt Martha left the South at a fairly young age following a career path that would land her in the United States Army. After being honorably discharged from service, she opted to take up residence in the Northern part of the Country in lieu of returning to the South. This distance resulted in us not seeing her much for long periods at a time yet when she visited we were supposed to be on our best behavior- of course good behavior for children was the norm when we grew up. Children really respected and honored their elder's even if they didn't know them. And of course, everyone had an active hand in helping to rear a child in those days.

For as long as I can recollect, Aunt Martha has always lived a respectful Christian life and her love for the Lord has been unquestionable. She began attending bible study early in life. She is among the oldest in her current church family where she has been an active member for well over 50 years. During this time she has assumed many roles in her dedicated service to our Savior. Assistant Sunday School Superintendent, Teacher, and President of the Missionary Ministry for 20 years just to name a few.

She was a devoted wife to Mr. Granderson Brown in a blessed union that spanned five decades before the Lord saw fit to call him from labor to reward in 2011. This amazing woman authored two other books prior to this current toil of love, living everyday to encourage and inspire all that she encounters.

So as you read this literary jewel that she has offered up as a testament of her undying worship to our Lord, I implore you to come to know this awesome God whom indeed has been her refuge in the time of trouble, her peace that surpasses all understanding, her friend that sticks closer than any brother, her supreme comforter and ultimate author and finisher of her tremendous faith.

Aunt Martha we love and adore you unwaveringly and we are super proud of what you've put your hand to the plow to do. Thank you for allowing your light to shine so brightly that both men and women have born witness to your marvelously good works and join us in glorifying our God in heaven.

Love, Your Niece
Bernyce Ishmael Sims
& Husband Theodore R. Sims

OUR DEAR AUNT MARTHA

Aunt Martha, You are an Inspiration to Our Family
Aunt Martha, you are our Special Inspiration
We count it all Joy and Bountiful Blessings from God
Each time we have an opportunity to be in your presence.
Your presence commands respect and honor
without you even speaking a word.
In your presence there is an opportunity
to observe and learn from you.
In your presence there is an opportunity
to listen and talk to you.

Aunt Martha, "Thank You" for the strong Christian, spiritual, loving, physical, mental, ethical, independent, moral and educational foundation that you helped to establish for our family.

Aunt Martha, you are our Living Legacy.

Aunt Martha, you have always been larger than life to us.
Aunt Martha, you have shown your love as a caring wife of Mr. Granderson Brown (our uncle) whom God created specially, specifically just for you.

You have demonstrated your Love towards your parents, siblings Ella, Metilda, Sallie, Cary, Eddie, Margaret, Louisa, Virginia and Frank all which are physically no longer with us.
Aunt Martha, it's because of you that we can continue to experience them through you.

Aunt Martha, you have blazed trails for others to follow by being the first female in the family to: (1) Graduate from Booker T. Washington High School as Salutatorian (Class of 1940), (2) Joined the U.S. Army (WWII 1943-1946), (3) Manager in the Claims Department at Blue Cross and Blue Shield and (4) Author of two (2) Books
and currently working on your third book.

Aunt Martha, "Thank You" for the barriers that you so gracefully and courageously challenged, penetrated and demonstrated during the course of your life time as only a God fearing Woman can do.

Aunt Martha, "Thank You" for being an example that we can readily see, talk to, hug, love on, touch, question, listen to and identify with by your experiences. We have witnessed the awesome, true and living power of God through your longevity and prosperous filled life and we are reminded of God's promise to never to leave us nor forsake us.

Aunt Martha, "Thank You" for giving us an opportunity to sincerely express how important you are to us as well as this family. We stand because of you and your accomplishments as a result of your strength. We walk on trails that you have blazed leading to unknown territory because of you and your accomplishments as a result of your tenacity.

Aunt Martha, we praise and glorify God for you and your accomplishments as well as the examples laid before us.

Aunt Martha, we "Thank You" for your prayers to an Omnipotent, Omnipresent and Omniscience God for our family. We all exist because of God's Love commended toward us through his only begotten Son, Jesus Christ. We are successful because of prayer warrior's like you and more specific God's Divine plan that He has for all of us.

Aunt Martha, you inspire others.
Aunt Martha, you encourage others.
Aunt Martha, you are highly appreciated.
Aunt Martha, many benefit from your Godly wisdom.
Aunt Martha, you are Loved Dearly.

Submitted by your nieces,
Karla & Mary
03 July 2012

Special Subjects / Women's Ministries

LIVING FROM THE INSIDE OUT
"Walking in the Newness of Life?
Freddie M. Lindsay-Payne

"Therefore we are buried with Him by baptism into death, that like as Christ was raised up from the dead by the glory of the Father even so we also should walk in newness of life." Romans 6:4

An interpretation of this Scripture is… "your old sin-loving nature was buried with Him by baptism when He died and when God the Father, with glorious power, brought Him back to life again, you were given His wonderful new life to enjoy.

Webster Dictionary's definition for a caterpillar is; as wormlike insect, brightly colored, hairy and spiny; a larvae, before metamorphosis. The newly hatched, earliest stage of any of various animals that undergo metamorphosis. The key factor here is (differing noticeably, in form and appearance from the adult).

Metamorphosis – is defined as a transformation, as by superhuman means. A marked alteration in appearance, condition character or function. A change in structure and habits during normal growth. It's the degeneration, irreversible deterioration of specific cells or organs. The dying away of cells and organs; sometimes resulting in death if it doesn't wait out its time.

Regeneration – is defined as an act or process of regenerating or state of being formed, reconstructed; undergoing a spiritual rebirth, revitalized, restored.

Paul states in Ephesians 4:23-24 that it is your attitudes and thoughts that must all be constantly changing for the better. You must be anew and different person, holy and good. You must be clothed with this new nature. A dead person, who died in the safety of Christ, has no desire for this world. So then, our perspective on our lives on earth should be elevated to a "heaven level" so that our lives will be an example of heavenly quality.

"Know that Christ died for us," states Romans 6:3-5, *"know ye not, that so many of us as were baptized into Jesus Christ were*

baptized in to his death? Therefore, we are buried with Him by baptism into death; that like as Christ was raised up from the dead by the glory of the Father, even so we also should walk in the newness of life. For if we have been planted together in the likeness of his death, we shall be also in the likeness of his resurrection. Now, if we be dead with Christ, we believe that we shall also live with him."

In the book of Corinthians, namely I Corinthians 15, Paul speaks of the seed that has to die in order to spring forth a beautiful blossom or produce a product. Paul says, let go of your old life and let God live through you. This is a surrendered life. This is a life of victory and blessing. *"Oh death where is thy sting? Oh grave, where is thy victory… thanks be to God who has given us the victory through our Lord Jesus Christ."*

In the newness of life, I am raised to a higher standard of living. I was condemned to sin, unable to do good, or be good. Now, when I became a Christian and strive to live a Christian life, I find it impossible to do – but, thanks be to God for faith and grace.

The word "I" is found 38 times in the seventh chapter of Romans, but it is not "I" that lives, but Christ that lives in me. Oh wretched man/woman that I am, who shall deliver me from the bond of sin?

When I step into an airplane, I am free from the law of gravity. The higher law operates as the plane lifts above the clouds. A few minutes earlier, the same gravity held me solidly to the earth. When I stepped into the plane, the law of gravity is not destroyed. But it becomes inoperative – under a different condition.

This is what happens in the newness of life, as we live from the inside out. The law that operates by the Spirit in my life lifts me above the world of sin so that sin no longer has dominion and power over me. It is inoperative. I am free. I am without condemnation.

We've got to get on the plane; the Jesus plane, and allow Jesus to take us far above evil principalities and powers. When you get pass chapter seven in Romans, and move to chapter eight, instead of the world "I" we find the word "Spirit": which is used 21 times.

There is no condemnation in Christ and no separation. Our life in Christ is safe for He is around us, the Spirit is in us, and God is for us.

> I want to be a follower of Christ.
> I want to be one of His disciples.
> I want to walk in the newness of life,
> So, let me be, a follower of Christ.
>
> What do I have to do?
> What do I have to say?
> How do I have to walk,
> Each and every day?
> Show me what does it cost,
> If I carry the cross?
> So let me be a follower of Christ.

Hymn: Follower of Christ
Baptist Hymnal

WOMEN FINDING FAVOR WITH GOD

In a book by Eugenia Price, author of *God Speaks to Women Today*, I quote these words.

> *"If humanity is to be purified and Christianized to a far greater extent than the present age, it is imperative to have an enlightened, spiritual womanhood."*

Isn't it interesting, then, that in the book of Proverbs, beginning in chapter eight, the writer refers to wisdom as a woman? I don't think anyone would deny the fact that men, children, other women and even pastors need the power that a wise woman possesses. I'm not exaggerating either! Just ask a few pastors.

When and if you study the bible, you will find examples of my declaration in examples like, Ruth, Jochebed, Deborah, Abigail, Esther, and Mary: all women who changed the course of history and found favor with God in their circumstances.

Isn't it also interesting that so many women in the Bible are never called by name? Why? I believe that God wants the spotlight to shine on what they did than on who they were. This is true for us as well.

By design, the Bible referenced 730 women who are unnamed and are examples for us. We might say the right words, speak the truth and never get praised, honored, or exalted. And although we might never get human recognition, it is ultimately important that as we journey through this life, we are able to find favor with God.

There are three very important points I would like to make:
- Our relationship with God
- Our relationship with people (women)
- Our relationship with ourselves

Your relationship with God is knowing that He is all: all powerful, all knowing, and Creator of us all. To find God's favor you must know that He is God – you are not!

Build your relationship on trusting Him and not yourself. Case closed! I can't trust myself to always do and say what is right. My tongue gets in the way. My emotions trip over themselves. I want to lead and not follow. I am full of envy and jealousy and I want to be right about everything. However, I trust God. I know that He is always right. I know that He can help me bridle my tongue. When I want to "bless" someone out, He helps me to "bless and praise His name." He gives me God-control. Jochebed, Hannah, and Mary all trusted God and He delivered. They found favor!

Let's look at point one: our relationship with God.

Jochebed was the mother of Moses. Despite Pharaoh's decree she could not harm her baby; so she hid him in her home at first. But then, after she could no longer hide him, she put Moses in an ark of bulrushes and laid him by the river bank trusting God for his life (Exodus 2:1-10).

Hanna, who held nothing back, wanted a baby. She prayed to God earnestly for a son, and promised to dedicate the child to His service. The book of 1 Samuel records her prayer of praise and her son's life of dedication to the Lord.

Mary was trusted with God's Greatest Gift. When informed by the angel of God's plan she simply asked, "How is this going to happen?" She never asked, "Are you sure," "Why me," or "What are people going to say about me"? Mary acquiesced, "Let it be to me according to your word" (Luke 1:39).

Point two: our relationship with other women.

"Entreat me not to leave you, or to turn back from following after you; for wherever you go, I will go; and wherever you lodge, I will lodge. Your people shall be my people and your God, my God. Where you die, I will die and there will I be buried. The Lord do so to me and more also, if anything but death parts you and me." Ruth 1:16-17

This is an example of a relationship with another woman; but the story does not end there. Boaz was the father of Obed and Ruth was his mother. Obed was the father of Jesse and 30 generations after them comes Jesus Christ, The Messiah; born of a woman named Mary. God was working and found favor with Ruth and Mary.

My third point: there is nothing better than a woman who knows who she is.

A woman who knows who she is will not accept trash, whether that trash is a bad relationship, a lie from the devil, who tells you that you can do anything you want, as long as you want without any consequences. A woman of God knows that He loves her. She knows that He has appointed her a destiny. A woman of God knows that He will provide appropriate human love and support; and she is wise enough to obey Him and be patient – and wait!

When a woman is walking in her calling, she is a walking epistle to the truth of God, and she is a powerful woman. But, women, your power is not in the volume of your voice; it's not in the mightiness of your actions; it's not in how many corporate boards you sit on; it's not in how many people ask for your advice; it's not in who you know and where you go; it's not in the chairwoman of the pastor's appreciation; it's not in the diamonds you wear on every finger. Your power is the precious name of Jesus; it's in knowing that Jesus died for us and made us all free – free from the domination of sin; delivered form Satan's takeover of your life.

Who are you? It's you who possesses the quiet beauty, the kind of beauty that does not brag or boast; the beauty that goes around doing good and never telling a soul. Peter talks about that beauty.

> "Do not let your beauty be that outward adorning of arranging the hair, or wearing gold, or of putting on fine apparel, but let it be the hidden person of the heart, with the incorruptible ornament of a gentle and quiet spirit, which is very precious in the sight of God" (1 Peter 3:4-5).

WALKING IN YOUR SEASON
Freddie M. Lindsay-Payne

II Timothy 4:1-4

Let's begin at the beginning and review where this writer, Paul, is and why he is writing this letter. Paul is in prison at Rome. He has had a productive and challenging life; a life in Christ that he is not afraid to talk about, both in the past and in the present. He writes to his son-in-the-gospel, Timotheus, who is involved in ministering; only Mark is with Paul at this time. There have been some struggles, some separations, many persecutions, some strange occurrences, but Paul is mentally right! He is where he wants to be in Christ at this season; he does not hesitate, however, to continue to bring everything into perspective, so he writes this letter to Timotheus.

Now, Timothy is and has been a faithful worker for Christ. Timothy did not have an earth moving story to tell about his conversion; he was not at a revival or tent meting when he got to know Christ. Timothy was blessed to have two strong women in his life; his grandmother and mother, Lois and Eunice. They brought him up in the nurture and knowledge of Christ and as a result of being in Christ; he was noticed by Paul and directed by God to become a minister of the gospel. In other words, Timothy was prepared when Paul met up with him. He was prepared and ready, in his season, to begin work.

Most of us like to do things when it is convenient for us. Not only do we want it convenient, but we want to do things on our own terms. Our season for accomplishing anything is when we get ready.

However, as we look at Paul's writing here in II Timothy 4, he stresses several points. <u>First Point</u> in verse #1, this is a time when God will judge us at his coming, at His appearance (a season). <u>Second Point</u> in verse #2, preach the gospel, in season and out of season. It wasn't convenient to God to send His Son, Jesus, into the world to die for our sins; but we were a messed up people on our way to hell without the possibility of recovery. So God sent His Son at a difficult time for mankind, but it was the season.

In a climate of moral ambivalence and confusion about moral values, the church's assignment is to make clear the content and the meaning of the gospel. We have so many diversions going on; issues demanding a response from God's chosen people – God's church. We have corporations that are interested in profit-making excesses (the gas crises); the abortion pro-choice and pro-life debate, genetic engineering and cloning. We're not satisfied with God's creation, we want to try and do it our way. Now we have several states that are ignoring God's law and creating their own with reproductive technologies and same sex marriage.

There is a clear and present danger permeating our lives and we are falling for it – hook, line, and sinker. We are chasing after myths and sensationalism. Christ never drew a crowd based on sensationalism. He drew a crowd based on the Word. However, we have crowds in some of our mega churches. For instance, Joel Olsteen draws big crowds, but Joel never goes to Calvary; never preaches Christ's death, never preaches hell is where we are going if we don't turn from our sin – and the center is packed.

I tell you that there is a clear and present danger season in our lives. In 2001, President Bush was told by his advisors that Osama Ben Laden and the region he controlled had weapons of mass destruction. Well, it was found out later, after the deaths of many American soldiers, that there were no weapons of mass destruction.

You are physically somewhere, right now! But God wants you on the move. Instead of praying "God, what do you want me to do next?" try asking, "God, what do you want me to do right now?"

We like to say, "Lord, if you send me I'll go." Well, you might not need to go anywhere. There is work to do right where you are. Directions from God are not just for your next big move. He has a purpose for you right now. He has placed you where He wants you.

How do we serve God in this season effectively? We must stop and take an inventory of ourselves. Where do you fit in the grand scheme of God's plan? God's purpose and plan for the Israelites was not just to transport a bunch of people from one land into another land. The journey for them was painful and hard – 40 years because of the condition of their hearts – a trip that should have taken only 11 days. God's purpose and plan was to teach them to live obediently. In the 40 years God taught and prepared them for the bigger picture.

Your spiritual journey may seem lengthy at times; it may not look like you are getting anywhere. Your life may be full of pain, discouragement and difficulties – but God isn't trying to make things easy for you. He's not just trying to keep you alive and give you a life. He is preparing you to live in service and devotion to Him. A little pain, a few discouraging words, some disappointments – all are season in our lives.

Let me convenience you today that you can be much more. But, you must peel off what is on the outside to get to the core – the good stuff. Like an onion, you must begin cutting away the outside, unusable covering. You must throw away that which cannot be used by God so you can get to self-control, perseverance, godliness, to sisterly and brotherly kindness and love.

"SISTA GIRL FRIEND"
(Written for Irene Heard)

You were always good at beating me at everything,
And here you have "won" again.
I could never keep up with you, so I just tried to do things for you.
Now, when I travel on the highways,
I won't have you to talk to me
from our beginning destination to the end.
I will, however, have the Lord on my side,
Just as He was with us on all of our trips.
No longer will I have the privilege of ironing your clothes
Getting ready for our Congress classes.
No longer will I have to worry about the TV being too loud,
Because you will be in Glory with our Lord.
I'll miss you so much!
No more salmon croquets, biscuits and jelly on the road.
No more frequent pit stops.
No more, "I'll pick you up! If you're not ready, I will wait.
No more talking about our children (and everybody else),
No more early (2 a.m.) departures and Momma Ella Mae fussing
about her crazy girls.
But there is one thing for sure,
I plan to join you one day and I'll be happy to see you.
However, until that day,
I'll make sure that I keep everything in order back here.
I'll make sure that I get Lee's dinner ready for him after work.
I'll make sure I look after the seniors at Warren Avenue.
I'll make sure that no one bothers your little "babies."
But do this one thing for me,
Save a seat for me so that we can talk to Apostle Paul together.
But most of all, "When I see Jesus!"
Amen

Love you, Freddie

Poetry

NOW IS THE TIME

Today if you will hear His voice and make Jesus your choice you will be wiser and have a greater impact on society. You will be able to:
Reach the unreachable
Teach the unteachable
Love the unlovable
Seek the unseekable
Rescue the perishable
Conquer the unconquerable
Think the possible
Reveal the revealable
Cheer the despicable
Bless the formidable
Rebuke the rebukable
Heal the brokenhearted
Love God supremely
Love others completely

Proclaim the message of salvation for the healing of the nation.

Anonymous

SPIRITUAL GROWTH

When I commune with my Lord and Savior
And sit at the great Gospel table
Multiple vitamins I do receive
To satisfy my bodily needs.

Getting prepared to battle with sin
To do my best some souls to win
No life can ever be fulfilled
Without true recognition of His will.

Pursuing righteousness in a world of strife
Praying constantly for a better life
Who can declare that living is vain
When so well sustained by His Holy name.

IF JESUS WOULD COME TO YOUR HOUSE

If Jesus would come to your house, to spend a day or two; if he came unexpectedly, I wonder what you'd do? Oh, I know you'd give your nicest room, to such an honored guest and all the food you'd serve him would be the very best. I know you would keep assuring him, you're glad to have him there; that serving him in your own home, is joy
beyond compare.

But when you saw him corning would you meet him at the door; With arms outstretched in welcome, to your heavenly visitor? Or would you have to change clothes before you let him in, or hide some magazines and put the Bible where they'd been? Would you turn off the radio and hope he hadn't heard, and wish you hadn't uttered, that last loud hasty word? Would you hide your worldly music and put some hymn books out instead? Oh! I wonder what you'd do if the Saviour came to spend a day or two with you.

Would you keep right on doing what you always do? Would you go right on saying the things you always say? Would your life continue as it does each and everyday? Would your family conversation keep its normal pace? Would you find it hard at mealtimes to say a table grace? Would you sing the songs you always sing, and read the books that you normally read, letting him know the kind of things on which your mind and spirit feed?

Would you take Jesus with you everywhere you'd plan to go? Or would you maybe change your plans for just a day or so? Would you be glad to have him meet your closest friends, or would you hope they'd stay away until his visit ends? Would you be glad to have him stay forever and ever on, or would you sigh with great relief when he at last was gone? It might be interesting to know, the things that you would do, if Jesus Christ in person came to spend some time with you.

Anonymous

"GO YE..."

It has been estimated that approximately 2,000,000 people lie down every night hungry in body; three out of every four lie down without God.

Christ's last message to His disciples was, "Go ye into all the world and preach the gospel to every creature."

It is the duty of every Christian--some day, in some way--to spread the gospel to those who have not heard it.

It is the duty of all Christians to give of time, money, prayer, and life itself, in some manner, for One who gave everything for them.

I was hungry, and you formed a humanities club and discussed my hunger. Thank you.

I was imprisoned and you crept off quietly to your chapel in the cellar and prayed for my release.

I was naked and in your mind you debated the morality of my appearance.

I was sick and you knelt and thanked God for your health.

I was homeless and you preached to me of the spiritual shelter of the love of God.

I was lonely and you left me alone to pray for me.

You seem so holy, so powerful, so close to God.
But I'm still very hungry and lonely and cold.

Anonymous

I LOVE YOU LORD! WHY?

I love you Lord! Why?
Because it was You not I
Who made my life worthwhile
Who saw my nothingness
Clothed me in your righteousness
Gave me a bit of worthiness
That I may receive some happiness.

I love you Friend! Why?
Because it was You not I
Who dried my tearful eyes
Who overlooked my shallowness
Saw in me some hopefulness
Wrapped me in your kindness
And relieved me of my blindness.

I love you Lord! Why?
Because it was You not I
Who for the whole world died
Without class or distinction
Without creed or reservation
Without hate or hesitation
That all may receive salvation.

I love you Lord! Why?
Because it was You not I
That heard my wayward cry
That healed my broken heart
That gave me an upward start
Prepared a home where Thou art
That I may live and never depart.

FOOTPRINTS ON PURPOSE

I want to leave some footprints
In the sand of time.
For I know that this life
Is not entirely mine.
It's mine to use as I live.
Sharing with others is never lost.
It is a gift from God above
And no one can count the cost.

WORKING

You are slowly building, working every day
Brick by brick, deeds and thoughts you lay
Building for the present, for the future too
Character that someday God Himself will view.

Anonymous

MORNING GRATITUDES

Good Morning Lord
Thank You for the wake up call
I can always depend on You
For recognizing the morning dew.

Good morning Dear Savior
Thank You for my state of behavior
I can choose the very best
And leave the squalid to the rest.

Good morning, Sustainer
How I know that Thou art able
To calm my fears, relieve my pains
And keep me in Thy Holy name.

My gratitudes are for my meals
The manner in which they do appeal
Grant that the body be well supplied
Be strengthened, be quick to others provide.

O what a glorious day
My sins have all been washed away
Now I am happy as can be
Knowing who has made me free.

ON BEING ACCEPTED BY OTHERS

What an enormous extent we go to be accepted by men
We bend and buckle as we listen to their whims
We shift from what's right to that which is wrong
To be an integral part of their invested throne
Is it really necessary to care so much
About what our peers think or about their lush?
What was wrong yesterday cannot be changed
Wealth and fame are transient, however, morals remain
We encounter misery for being a part of their in-thing
It is possible to be caught up in a whirlwind of sin
Before we realize we should have taken a stand
For that is what maturity and Christianity demand.
We have to live with our conscience and face facts
In the end it matters not what one thinks of that
Remember freedom to think and act as you please
Is a God-given personality which will put you at ease.

WHAT SHALL I RENDER?

What shall I render
For all His benefits to me
What shall I render
Since Christ has set me free?

What shall I render
Since He has made me whole
What shall I render
Shall I offer gifts of gold?

What shall I render
Since He has given me sight
What shall I render
Shall I serve with all my might?

What shall I render
To the One who is Lord indeed
What shall I render
Since He supplies my need?

What shall I render
For the extension of my life
What shall I render
For relieving me from strife?

What shall I render
For family and friends of God
What shall I render
Since He is Lord of lords?

I shall cling to what is right
And hold a brighter light
Share freely, give praise and adoration
For His marvelous work of salvation.

OPEN MINE EYES

O God, open mine eyes that I may see
The task that Thou hast given to me

To do my best with all my might
And look to Thee for strength and light.

I dare not think how I have shirked
Or drifted away from Thy manifold work

Please forgive my failures, renew my mind
Committed to Thee, I would be thine.

Forgetting myself and reaching for others I cannot see
Thee without my brother Frail as I am I come to Thee
From selfish desires please set me free.

MORNING THANKFULNESS

Come with the morning hour
It's time to kneel and pray
Dear God, we thank Thee for all things
Especially an endless day.

In humility and sincerity we come, To
praise Thee for Thy Son;
For gracious friends and ruthless opponents
And all the victories won.

Starting with Thee is such a delight
Whatever duty or task assigned,
May be considered a blessing
And not with neglect or resigned.

May we remember Thy goodness true
Before the closing of our eyes
Forgive us for our many sins
Sweet peace and rest besides.

How great it is to trust Thy Word
To live in love sublime.
From everlasting Thou art God
In all Thy ways divine.

THE DESIRABLE GIFT

It's almost indescribable
Yet so very reliable
It's the gift of the Holy Bible.

It's easy to talk
Somewhat difficult to walk
Reluctant to complain or balk.

It sends forth projections
Regardless of races or connections
There are no such things as rejections.

It cannot be hidden
Or ever bed-ridden
Being fully decked and glidden.

May be found in the young and old
Age is a factor untold
It's forever to have and to unfold.

There's plenty to give
As long as you live
Easy to admit wrong and to forgive.

It cannot be still
While full of good will
No problem to climb up a hill.

It's a dynamic power
For every crucial hour
An ever soaring tower.

It's a source of inner peace
Combined with joy replete
To all within its reach.

It is activated Love
Which comes from God above
The most desirable gift with the
Seal of a heavenly dove.

WHOM SHALL I SEND?

Whom shall I send?
Who is willing to go?
The Lord has need of workers
And not for just a show.

Go into the wretched world
The fields are truly white
Where so many are perishing
In need of that saving light.

See precious lives being wasted
In search of wealth and fame,
Some in despair and lack direction
Devoid of His glorious name.
Take the gospel message
Tell of our Savior's love
How he came to save us
From the curse that was incurred.

O the wonderful bountiful blessings
He will gladly bestow
Upon those who will trust Him
And promote kingdom building below.
Whom shall I send?
Who will heed and answer the call?
Our Lord is still pleading
As He extends this outreach to all.

MEETING THE STANDARD

God's work is not on production
It cannot be done with reluctance
In order to reach the specific mark
Sincere desires must come from the heart.
If you try to make an impression
And do it using your own discretion
You will fail to meet the standard
By diverting from the proper angle.
There's so much that should be done
Before the race on earth is run
Consider well and give your best
This is where the promises rest.

Some would be seen and heard
Full of life and flowery words
Our Lord is not interested in these
Neither in one who does as he pleases.
But what does the Lord require?
To do justly, love mercy, worldly pleasures deny,
Always walk humbly in His sight
To obtain blessings, strength and might.

APPRECIATION

A word of appreciation to a special person
A bit of encouragement too,
For services rendered and even more
To show we care about you.
How much we care cannot be measured
In gifts, words or time
But efforts are to impart some joy
From grateful hearts to thine.
What seemed a success or victory
Was not always met with a smile,
Now you can be reassured
Each noble task was worthwhile.
Something you considered a failure
May have caused you deep regret,
Through many adverse circumstances
You can find true happiness.
Accept this as a temporary token
From those whose purses are thin
And now we wish you greater rewards
With bliss that never ends.

FRAGILITY OF MAN

A frequent question of whence cometh man?
A careful design of the Master's hand
Poor silent form of earthly clay
Waiting for the break of day.

Nothing in his hands he brings lifeless,
depending creature for everything; helpless,
knowing not from whence he came
Not even a mind and no one to blame.

Feet he had but could not walk
Thickened tongue that could not talk
Bodily movements still at ease
Internal organs in earthly freeze.

Brain he had but could not think
Eyes in place without a wink
Into the nostril the God of life breathed
Permitting man to function rightly or as he pleased.

God gave a beautiful body and sacred mind
To an inanimate object like none of its kind
Wisdom, knowledge and Plan of Salvation,
Dominion and power to rule over nations.

What gracious loving Fatherly choice
To give a simple innocent man a voice
In matter of life and death to decide
Eternity in heaven or hell to reside.

DISTRESSED MOMENT

Why are you weeping?
You're still in God's keeping
When you remember His Word
Your heart will be encouraged.

Tho you cannot be still
Ask if it is His will
Then count it a blessing
To be learning a lesson.

Your heart may be weak
Your spirit so meek
Your body may shake
And how you must ache!

When your health is involved
Your body is the Lord's
Let Him have His way
Yield over and pray.

YOUTHS WAIT

At the crossroad of life they wait
Stranded-but not for long
Somewhat bewildered and often confused
Seeking which road to take home.

Some friendly faces with great concern
Magnificent plans and instant dreams
Waiting to get started in a fantastic world
To accomplish their fullest means.

Greater decisions in life awaits
It's time to depart from tic-tac-toe,
Cheer up and your balance regain
A slip of the foot you cannot let go.

Someone must help the stranded travelers
To cross the dangerous road secure
Surely no one can fail them
As they pass the crisis stage below.

The roads are frequently crowded
Impatient tailgaters shun
Be not persuaded to join the rank
Take time to think there's much to learn.

Learn to be courteous, loving and kind
Take the highway that leads to the right
The King has proclaimed it is the best
It's straight and full of lights.

Take refuge in His Holy Word
If obstacles come your way
No need to fear, He will be your guide
Leading safely to an endless day.

MOTHER'S INFLUENCE

Mother-sweetest person on the earth
How I loved your gentle touch,
Kindly acts and gracious too
O how much I owe to you!

You taught me how to work and play
Never to forget the honest way,
I remembered well the family prayers
Everyone knew God planted you there.

You cared so much, but not too much,
To give an occasional brushing up
Knowing that discipline was required
Children are better with rules applied.

What seemed a success was met with a smile.
Of course, each task was labeled worthwhile
If defeat or failure entered the path,
Encouragement was offered, dismay could not last.

In days when no longer your face I see.
The pleasant memories still linger with me
My life projects what mother taught
The handwork reflects an image wrought.

I'm so happy God loaned us to each other
With bounty blessings, with sisters and brothers
When all have been said and all things done
We'll be together when the victory is won.

AN EVENING PRAYER

Dear Lord, we come before thy throne
Seeking forgiveness for all our wrong
Thanking thee for all thou hast done
From early morn till setting of sun.

For all your constant provisions for life
For preventing us from engaging in strife,
For the opportunities to be kind to others
And the blessings of sisters and brothers.

Thanks for things seemingly not in our favor
But Lord we know how Thou art able
To sprinkle our lives with sunshine and rain
That we may be able to praise your name.

Thank you for keeping us while we sleep
That we may receive your inner peace
Our sincere gratitudes are forever yours
Thank you again that this day is closed.
Amen!

THE EVER-PRESENT LORD

What joys there are to know the Lord
To feast upon His precious
Word To drink from His fountain of life
To live in love instead of strife.
A peacemaker He is in perilous time
A comforter to a troubled mind;
In loneliness an ever present friend
Who promised to keep us to the end.

When home life seems out of control
And poverty or misery is what you behold;
Blessings are plentiful, if you'll only be still
Pray, trust and obey the Master's Will.
O God, we thank you for the depths of your love
For Jesus Christ from heaven above
For all our needs, He does supply
Please help us on Him more to rely.

May we but share with our fellowmen
The Good News of our Savior, and then
Your call we must answer and no more roam
We pray for sweet rest in our heavenly home.

BEATITUDES OF THE AGED

Blessed are they who understand
my faltering step and shaking hands.

Blessed are they who know that my ears today
must strain to catch the words they say.

Blessed are they that know
my eyes and my wits are slow.

Blessed are they that look away
when my cup of coffee spilled today.

Blessed are they with a cherry smile
who stop to chat with me for a while.

Blessed are they who say
"You've told that story twice today."

Blessed are they who know the way
to bring back lovely yesterdays.

Blessed are they that made it known
that I am loved not left alone.

Blessed are they who know the loss
of strength I need to bear the cross.

Blessed are they who ease the days
on my home in loving ways.

Anonymous

HYPOCRITICAL SINGING

The singing of a hymn should be a great experience. It can be a prayer, a testimony, a praise or an invitation. Someone has written some interesting comparisons regarding the hymns we sing:

We sing "Sweet Hour of Prayer"
    and content ourselves with five or ten minutes daily.
We sing "Onward Christian Soldier"
    and wait to be drafted into service.
We sing "Oh for a Thousand Tongues"
    and don't use the one we have for God.
We sing "There Shall Be Showers of Blessings"
    but do not come to church when it is raining.
We sing "Blest Be the Tie That Binds"
    and let the least little offense sever it.
We sing "Serve the Lord With Gladness"
    and complain about all we have to do.
We sing "We're Marching to Zion"
    but fail to march to Church.
We sing "I Love to Tell the Story"
    and never mention it to a neighbor
We sing "Cast Thy Burden On the Lord"
    and worry ourselves into nervous breakdowns
We sing "The Whole Wide World For Jesus"
    and never invite our neighbors to church.
We sing "0 Day of Rest and Gladness"
    and wear ourselves out traveling.
We sing "Throw Out the Life Line"
    and content ourselves with throwing out a fishing line.

Anonymous

PENSIVE MOOD

At the close of a very busy day
The time to toss my cares away
To check the records of what I've done
From early morn to setting sun

Have I completed all of the tasks assigned
Perhaps, there's more I had in mind;
Did I forget to wash some feet
Or failed some stranger in the gate to greet?

Have I done what the Lord requires
Or satisfied with my own desires?
What should be my greatest concern
Of all the lessons I sought to learn?

I am accountable to my Lord and King
For wise use of time, influence and everything
I pray that when I've done my best
I will close my eyes in peaceful rest.

THY WILL BE DONE!!
(Dedicated to my niece, Willette Jackson)
In memory of a loving sister

Thy will, **O** Lord, not mine!
How can I say it at a time
When burdens are heavy, spirit low
And life is different from what I know?

Thy will, **O** Lord, I cry, I cry.
When trouble comes I cannot deny
Thou art still upon the sacred throne
Perceiving all that's right and wrong.

How can I say I love you, Lord
When I am so desperately short on call?
How can I really do what is right
When so many things obscure my sight?

How can I say thank you for pain
Or say thy will be done when little remain?
How can I sing praises to Thee for good
When I have stood as much as I could?

What shall I say when without a friend?
Thy will I cry I'll see her again
Thou knowest what is always best
I must remain to stand the test.

Thy will, thy will I must employ
Who measures our tears as well as joy?
Into thine hands I am just a mold
The rest of my life you will unfold.

CROSSING OVER

The battle of life has been fought
A crown of life has been won
I am thankful the struggle is over
And for a glorious welcome home.

I have met my loving Savior
Whose Word I've long proclaimed
And joined the heavenly host
Singing Glory to His name.

You can't imagine the newly discovered joy
Of leaving the world behind
No tears, no pain - just peaceful rest
And all is supremely divine.

Dear Family, I wish not to leave you
But surely you will recall;
That time must meet its fulfillment
And grim reaper death will claim us all.

We'll meet again some sweet day
In mansions that have been prepared
Just keep the faith and trust His Word
I promise, I promise to meet you there.

TRUE FRIENDSHIP

Is not found in what one thinks
Nor what one really does
The essence of true friendship
Is in scope of how one loves

The possibility of turning the world upside down
Simply would be no earthly good
If done to manifest selfish concern
Just doing it because you could

Endurance of these are short when hurt
Somewhat like tinkling cymbal or sounding brass
When the heart and the mind are not in tune
The invested harmony will not last

A friend will love always
Will certainly remain in spite of faults
Looking closely at the life of each other
Discovering no one is complete as he ought

True friendship is a rich possession
A prize commodity that cannot be bought
A rare and precious gift
That is abstract and cannot be taught

A ray of hope when the day is completed
An encouraging smile when the world is cold
When lonely there warmth of a friend
With abundance of kindness and more to behold

When all is said and finally done
In fair weather as well as blustering night
You cannot be left in utter darkness
When surrounded by one who holds a light.

GOD'S LITTLE SQUIRRELS

Around our house were two little squirrels
Prancing around in their own dandy world
Engaging happily in work and play
Squirming and fiddling as onward they sway

Dressed meticulously in brownish yellow
Oh, you should see these little fellows
If it were possible to know their thoughts
Amazement would be generated as what is wrought

It is fascinating to watch them run
From structure to structure in eager fun
With much rapidity, yet careful to flee
From life threatening danger to position in tree

Comes a time when there is little to eat
They sit near the door in stately manner on feet
Pleading for a bit of your worldly goods
Desiring you share as much as you would

If you toss them something, away they go
How quickly they come back for more?
If peanuts are given, there seems to be a grin
Hidden in the earth and seldom found again

These little creatures remind me of others
Higher creatures but they don't look further
Who after having received great blessings
Store them away without learning a lesson

Putting treasures in bags with holes
Or burying them in earthly fold
They cannot live like the little squirrels
But must be accountable in a different world.

IS ANYBODY HAPPIER...?

Is anybody happier because you passed his way?
Des anyone remember that you spoke to him today?

The day is almost over, and its toiling time is through;
Is there anyone to utter now a kindly word of you?

Can you say tonight, in parting with the day that's slipping fast,
That you help a single brother of the many that you passed?

Is a single heart rejoicing over what you did or said?
Does the man whose hopes were fading,
now with courage look ahead?

Did you waste the day or lose it? Was it well or sorely spent?
Did you leave a trail of kindness, or a scar of discontent?

As you close your eyes in slumber, do you think that God will say,
"You have earned one more tomorrow by the work you did today"?

Anonymous

Dramatics

IN THE BEGINNING
Light & Darkness

One Older Child with a large flashlight who keeps it on throughout the presentation or standing lights on.

Seven smaller or younger children carrying smaller flashlights. Assemble in the rear of the auditorium and march in singing, "Jesus Is The Light."

Auditorium, somewhat in darkness. Kaleidoscopic or flood light permissible.

Memorization emphasizing key words will enhance the sacredness of the drama.

OLDER CHILD: "In the beginning was the <u>Word</u> and the <u>Word</u> was with <u>God</u> and the Word was God. The same was in the beginning with God. In Him was life and the life was the <u>light</u> of men. The light shineth in the darkness; and the darkness could not prevent it from shining.

ALL: And it was so! (Turn lights on leaving on for the approximate count of ten; turn all lights off simultaneously.)

OLDER CHILD: In the beginning God created the heaven and the earth. The earth was without definite form and was uninhabited. <u>The Spirit of God moved</u> upon the face of the waters. God said, "Let there be light."

ALL: And there was <u>light!</u> God was pleased with it! (Lights on and off as in action one.)

OLDER CHILD: God saw the light that it was good, divided it from the darkness; calling the light Day and the darkness Night.

ALL: The evening and morning were the first day. (Lights on and off).

OLDER CHILD: God said, "Let there be a space in the midst of the water."

ALL: So it was as He spoke. (Lights on and off.)

OLDER CHILD: He also divided the waters that were under the space from the waters which were above; calling the space above <u>Heaven</u>. The evening and the morning were the second day.

ALL: So it was day two as He said. (Repeat lights.)

OLDER CHILD: God said, "Let the waters under the Heaven be gathered together into one place and let the dry land appear." The dry land He called Earth and waters Seas.

ALL: Immediately this became a reality! (Repeat lights.)

OLDER CHILD: Having accomplished this, He commanded the earth to bring forth grass; seed-bearing plants, fruit trees with seeds inside the fruit so that these seeds would produce the kinds of plants and fruits they came from.

ALL: So it was day three with growth on the earth which pleased God. (Repeat lights.)

OLDER CHILD: On the fourth day, God commanded the sun, moon and stars into existence to preside over day and night; to bring about seasons and to mark days and years.

ALL: So it was! Praise God! (Repeat lights.)

OLDER CHILD: On the fifth day, God filled the waters abundantly with moving creatures that had life and winged fowl after its kind. God blessed them saying, "Be fruitful and multiply, fill the waters in the seas and let the fowl multiply in the earth.

ALL: Truly it was so! (Repeat lights.)

OLDER CHILD: On the sixth day, God said, "Let the earth bring forth the living creature after his kind, cattle and creeping thing and beast of the earth after his kind.

ALL: So it was and God saw that it was good! (Repeat lights.)

OLDER CHILD: God climaxed His creation on the sixth day with the formation of man from the dust of the ground; breathed into his nostril the breath of life and man became a living soul. He was made in the image of God with a three-fold nature physical, mental and spiritual.

The Lord God caused a deep sleep to fall upon Adam and a rib was taken from him which He created Adam's help meet, Eve. God blessed them saying, "Be fruitful, multiply and replenish the earth and subdue it: and have dominion over the fish of the sea, and over the fowl of the air, and over every living thing that moveth upon the earth."

ALL: Thus ended the creation and God saw everything that He had made and declared it was very good. Hallelujah! (Repeat lights.)

OLDER CHILD: Out of the unknown comes the known, out of darkness comes light, out of ignorance comes knowledge; out of emptiness comes fullness, out of strife comes love.

Truly the Lord is our Light and our Salvation who is always available to lead us into the path of righteousness – now, henceforth and forever. Amen!

ALL: Amen! Amen! Amen!

Lights remain on as all exit singing, "Jesus Is the Light." (To highlight the occasion, an individual may be designated to display large numbers identifying each day in orderly procession.)

THE TEN COMMANDMENTS WRITTEN AND COMMANDMENTS APPLIED

Prepared by
Ruth Isabel & Martha Brown
Characters: Portrayer of the Voice of God
(Seated in balcony or unseen area)
Moses
Narrator
Aaron
Miriam, the prophetess
Elders (3 persons)
Multitude of People
Reader (Background Information)

Theme Song: **"Let My People Go"**

Sceneries of the children of Israel at Mt. Sinai

Reader: From the time God gave Eve to Adam in the Garden of Eden and said to them, "Be fruitful, and multiply, and replenish the earth," there have been special commandments to follow for successful living. They began with a simple test of obedience, progressed to covenants and culminated into the Ten Commandments for a chosen people. The failure of men to obey God has not only met with serious consequences, but often resulted in annihilation.

Operating one's life without God is similar to operating a car without oil; one will eventually encounter serious functional problems. As we endeavor to present "The Ten Commandments Written and Commandments Applied", we pray that you may be ever mindful of the Great Commander-in-Chief of all lives – Almighty, All powerful, Always present, sees and knows all things.

Narrator: The children of Israel, having been delivered out of Egypt from under the bondage of Pharaoh, crossed the Red Sea on dry land, entered into the wilderness and are now approaching Mt. Sinai. (While this is being narrated, Moses with the leaders and children of Israel slowly enter.) Let My People Go" (singing)

Narrator: And Moses went up unto God and the Lord called unto him out of the mountains.(Moses leaves multitude and enters highest level of the choir stand.)

Voice of God: Thus shalt thou say to the house of Jacob, and tell the children of Israel; ye have seen what I did unto the Egyptians and how I bore you on eagles' wings and brought you unto myself. Now, therefore, if ye will obey my voice indeed and keep my covenant, then ye shall be a peculiar treasure unto me above all people; for all the earth is mine.

(Moses comes down to the people and call for the Elders)

Moses: Elders, the Lord has said that ye have seen what I did unto the Egyptian, and how I bore you on eagles' wings and brought you unto myself. Now, therefore, if ye will obey my voice indeed and keep my covenant, then ye shall be a peculiar treasure unto me above all people; for all the earth is mine.

People: All that the Lord hath spoken we will do. (Moses returns to the mount.)

Voice of God: Lo, I come unto thee in a thick cloud, that the people may hear when I speak with thee, and believe thee forever. Go unto the people and sanctify them today and tomorrow, and let them wash their clothes, and be ready on the third day; for the third day the Lord will come down in the sight of all the people upon Mount Sinai. And thou shalt set bound unto the people round about saying, Take heed to yourselves, that ye go not up unto the mount, or touch the border of it. Whosoever toucheth the mount shall be surely put to death.

Narrator: And Moses went down from the mount unto the people, and sanctified the people; and they washed their clothes.

(Moses comes down and speaks to the Children of Israel)

Moses: Be ready on the third day. Don't go near your wives.

(Move off stage slowly. Solo. Return to stage.)

Narrator: And it came to pass on the third day in the morning, that there were thunders and lightnings, and a thick cloud upon the mount, and the voice of the trumpet exceedingly loud, so that all the people that were in the camp trembled.

Moses: Come ye out to the foot of the mountain to meet God.

(Moses ascends to the upper level. Thunder roars, trumpet sounds and lightning flashes. Moses remains through this to talk with God.)
(Music)

Moses: The people cannot come up to Mount Sinai; for thou chargest us, saying Set bounds about the mount and sanctify it.

Voice of God: Away, get thee down, and thou shalt come up, thou and Aaron with thee; and let not the priests and the people break through to come up unto the Lord, lest he break forth upon them.

Narrator: And Moses went down unto the people and spoke unto them. (Solo or Song)

(Following this, Moses returns mid level with Aaron)

Voice of God: (Commandments are given from Exodus 20:2-17).

(People become terrified, move slowly away from the Mount, and finally off stage.)
"I Am Bound For the Promised Land" (Singing)

THE TEN COMMANDMENTS APPLIED
Part II
Characters: Portrayer of Christ
Narrator
Rich Young Ruler
Pharisees & Scribes-2 of each
Man with withered hand
Woman taken in adultery
Temple Group of 4 or 5 persons

Narrator: God has constantly manifested His loving kindness and tender mercies to man in spite of man's proneness to disobedience and idolatry. The law with all its harsh penalties; often resulting in death was not a deterrent to crime. Social, moral and spiritual degeneration prevailed. Those responsible for the administration of the law were sometimes the worst perpetrators. No end was seen to oppression. The law did not establish justice; it made man aware of sin and served as a schoolmaster to bring him to Christ.

When the fullness of time had come, God sent His only begotten Son into the world to redeem man from the curse of the law and also to change his destiny.

In this portion of the Ten Commandments, our intent is to show the relationship of Jesus to the Commandments, His interpretation of them and the application to individual lives.

The scenes being dramatized are those involving the moral, spiritual and physical aspects of the law. Tune in now to the teaching of Jesus Christ in the temple as emphasis is placed on His superiority and authority over the law.

Portrayer of Christ: (Speaking from a seated position) Think not that I am come to destroy the law or the prophets; I am not come to destroy, but fulfill. Whosoever therefore shall break one of these commandments, and shall teach men to, he shall be called the least in the kingdom of heaven; and whosoever shall do and teach them, the same shall be called great in the kingdom of heaven.

(Enter scribes and Pharisees escorting the woman taken in adultery, seating her in the midst of those in the temple. One scribe and a Pharisee escorting her while the second scribe and second Pharisee follow closely.)

1st Pharisee: Master, this woman was taken in adultery. We caught her in the very act.

1st Scribe: Moses commanded that such should be stoned; but what sayest thou? (Portrayer of Christ stoops down and with his finger writes on the ground as though he hears them not.)

2nd Scribe: What shall we do, stone her? (Stands the woman up and lifts stone as if he is ready for action.)

2nd Pharisee: You know it is the law, how can you ignore it? I wonder if he thinks he is better than Moses who gave us the law. Shall we stone her? (Loudly)

Portrayer of Christ: (Stands up) He that is without sin among you, let him first cast a stone at her. (Again, he stoops down and writes on the ground.) (The would-be convictors leave one by one looking downward, condemned by their own conscience.)

Portrayer of Christ: Stands up, looks around and seeing none except the woman, speaks directly to her) Woman, where art thou accusers? Hath no man condemned thee?

Woman: No man, Lord. (Submissively)

Portrayer of Christ: Neither do I condemn thee; go and sin no more.

(Woman goes away rejoicing for the forgiveness of sin.) Solo "He Touched Me"

Narrator: Thank God for the forgiveness of sin! What if Moses, David, Solomon, the woman at the well and many others had received the penalty of the law for their sins? Christ, in His Infinite Wisdom is still using unworthy men and women as instruments in kingdom building.

Let us learn another message from the encounter of Christ with the rich young ruler.

(Enter young rich ruler.)

Young Rich Ruler: Good Master, what good things shall I do that I may have eternal life?

Portrayer of Christ: Why callest thou me good? There is none good but one, that is God; but if thou wilt enter into life, keep the commandments.

Rich Ruler: Which?

Portrayer of Christ: Thou shalt do no murder, thou shalt not commit adultery, thou shalt not steal, thou shalt not bear false witness. Honor thy father and thy mother; and thou shalt love thy neighbor as thyself.

Rich Ruler: All these have I kept from my youth up. What else do I need? (Speaks with great self-esteem and assurance.)

Portrayer of Christ: If thou wilt be perfect, go and sell what thou hast, and give to the poor, and thou shalt have treasure in heaven; and come and follow me.

(Rich Ruler goes away looking sad, very much dejected).

Narrator: In Matthew, Chapter 19:16-30, Jesus repeated five of the original Ten Commandments, added a sixth, "Thou shalt love thy neighbor as thyself," thus summarizing the six commandments which deal with man's relationship to each other. Three other commandments, those concerning man's relationship to God are not specified; however, they are well defined in the refusal of the rich man to follow Christ.

Loving one's family or possessions more than Christ is an idol. Calling Christ a good man, a good teacher, the man upstairs, or any other name devoid of recognition as the Son of God is tantamount to taking the name of the Lord in vain.

(Music)

(Scene shifts to the healing of man with withered hand)

Portrayer of Jesus is in the temple teaching and is being watched by Pharisees and Scribes, Luke 6:6-12.

Portrayer of Christ: (Walks over to man.) Rise up, and stand forth in the midst. (Man rises and stands)

Portrayer of Christ: (Speaking to Pharisees and Scribes) Is it lawful on the Sabbath days to do good or to do evil; to save life or to destroy it? (After looking round about, he said to the man) Stretch forth thy hand.

(Man stretches forth his hand and with second glance realizes it is healed, rejoices)

Narrator: Before this healing, Jesus had told the Pharisees that He was Lord of the Sabbath. Christ rose on the first day of the week and the early disciples began to observe this as a testimony to His Lordship. The important question to answer, is He Lord of your life? Then each day is a special observance to Him in love and service.

Jesus Christ summed up the commandments; Thou shalt love the Lord thy God with all thy heart, and with all thy soul, and with all thy mind, and with all thy strength; this is the first commandment. The second is this: Thou shalt love thy neighbor as thyself. There is no other commandment greater than these.

Let us hear the conclusion of the whole matter: Fear God, and keep His commandments; for this is the whole duty of man.

RACING WITH FATHER TIME

Scriptural Introduction Portion of Ecclesiastes Chapter 3: To every thing there is a season, and time to every purpose under the heaven: A time to be born, a time to die; a time to plant, and a time to pluck up that which is planted; a time to weep, and a time to laugh; a time to mourn, and a time to dance; a time to embrace, and a time to refrain from embracing; a time to get, and a time to lose...

He has made every thing beautiful in his time; also he has set the world in their heart, so that no man can find out the work that God maketh from the beginning to the end...

I know that there is no good in them, but for a man to rejoice, and to do good in his life. And also that every man should eat and drink, and enjoy the good of all his labour, it is the gift of God.

PART I
Character Portrayals:
Father Time, Betty, Mother Nature, Jimmy
A neighbor, Stella

Theme Song: **"Life's Railway to Heaven"**
Costumes: Those of Mother Nature & Father Time may be somewhat old fashioned; others more contemporary.

Setting: Living room of the Times displaying a sofa, chairs, table, floor lamp, bookcase, wall picture and flowers.

This two part drama correlates time and opportunities as active forces in the lives of people, especially, young people. They are either molded into constructive beings by right decisions or fragmented by the forces of wrong decisions. Involved in both parts are a Choral Group and a Soloist.

PART I

(Father Time sits comfortably on sofa while Mother toys around with furniture. Children act as if they are engaged in a study period). Soft Music: Chorus of Theme Song

Father Time: I am the captain of all I survey and the human master of all that pass my way. I usher individuals into the vast universe of opportunities, maintain a firm clutch on them and demand nothing in return. (Speaking somewhat boastfully)

It is you individually who must learn to run or to walk; to crawl or to talk; to work or to shirk; to love or to hate; to choose or to wait. These things I cannot do for you, but I can reassure you (waves hands) that I will be around because I am Father Time. Don't forget I will be around: In spite of what may happen, I will see you through.

Mother Nature: (Attention on family). Being the proud mother of human existence, I am delighted to nourish, cherish, teach, discipline, sustain and set forth excellent standard for living. It is mother who cares, caresses, wipes away tears and smiles when things go wrong. Ask me who drapes, shakes and make hearts leap for joy? Who whisper words of cheer in face of fear? Who sings as darkness appears? Who welcomes the rebel home? Yea, it is Mother who pretends you can do no wrong because you are so near and dear to her heart.

Betty: Mom, you are great! Life seems so dull, (speaking seriously) so boring and sometimes useless. Tell me, do you have a recipe for success or a magic formula for happiness? Looks as if something should be done about the public school system. Twelve years plus for basic education in addition to coping with other circumstances and interest. What happens if one decides to enter college or attend a vocational school? Studying takes so much joy out of life. The beat goes on, on and on.

Jimmy: I agree with you Betty, not just one hundred – but wo hundred per cent. In as much as everything else is legislated, why not six months of school and six months vacation? Kids would be just as well off. I have seen so much in my many years of living (smiles). Just think of the dropouts, fallouts, shootouts, knockouts, kickouts, and don't mention the burnt out children; all physically and mentally handicapped. Something should be done to prevent some of these disasters.

Father Time: Trying to escape the main stream of life and that which will remain with you ... The school of learning. I tell you, it cannot be done. My suggestion is to reduce your speed. How can you travel sixty miles an hour in a restricted zone in a Model "T" car? Either you will not reach your destination or your destination will reach you unexpectedly. Slow down and live! In other words ... consider your body, the time in which you live and your abilities.

Soloist: **"Life's Railway to Heaven."**

Betty: Lovely! Simply Wonderful! Am I looking forward to the sweetest melodies of living? Can hardly wait until I am eighteen, out of school and doing my own thing (Somewhat bashful). Of course, I mean in a decent way.

Mother Nature: How you children think! (Holding head as if in distress) Agonizing over yesterday, complaining about today and building castles for tomorrow. Who knows what a day will bring? We have taught you the importance of patience. We admonish you to wait, to love, to work; to set definite goals for the future; to think of others instead of self. Happiness does not consist of what you get but what you give. The joy of living comes from the inner self and projects itself without.

Jimmy: It would be great to enjoy life at a young age, when you are handsome, full of vigor and vitality. I had rather be working when I am older than the younger years because there is a possibility of being slowed down by some crippling condition or wasting disease.

Choral Group: **"Wait on the Lord."**

(Door bell rings, Mother Nature answers and Stella enters)

Stella: Hello everyone! Had not seen you in quite a while, therefore, I decided to stop by. My recent check on others in the neighborhood indicates no real problems. Drifting along with the tides as usual.

Mother Nature: Fine!

Jimmy: We have decided to check in the library before going out for a little tennis competition. If it's OK... (looking at both parents) we will see you later?

Betty: (Hugs Mother) Anything you want done, or shall I pick up some things on my way home?

Mother Nature: I believe we are fairly well supplied. Please be careful.

Betty: Make sure you take good care of dad and keep him awake until we return (smiles, waves and departs).

Mother Nature: (Turning to Stella) What's new, Stella?

Stella: Nothing unusual. Busy as a bee and extending myself almost as thinly as a flea. Before one particular project is resolved another is in progress. We are desperately in need of counselors and supporters for our young people. Is at all possible for you to host a group from our District Council, Saturday morning at ten o'clock for a rap session?

Mother Nature: I would love to do so. Please call me later with additional information regarding the group, their activities and the number anticipated.

Stella: Thank heaven! An answer to my prayer. I love you dearly! Will call tomorrow. (Waves gently) Have a great day!

Choral Group: (To be selected)

End of Part One
(INTERMISSION: May be used as an offertory period)

RACING WITH FATHER TIME
PART II

<u>Character Portrayals:</u>
Mary Haste, Mother Nature, Johnny Waste, Father Time
Leon & Latrice Beaver, Betty, Youth Counselor, Stella,
Jimmy, Theresa & Daughter, Patricia

(Home of the Times during an informal meeting of Young People)

Stella: Feel free to express your opinion on issues. It is this avenue of communication that enhances our relationship also enables us to recognize problems and seek solutions.

Leon: Latrice and I fortunately have a marvelous marital relationship and have found meaning and purpose in life because of our personal fellowship with the body of Christ. However, recently I have not experienced the spiritual growth anticipated. It's ironic that the barriers seem to be social and economics. We are not concerned so much about having everything the Joneses have... but some things. We are determined to hang in there.

Latrice: True. Friends are not receptive to our lifestyle and we cannot be partakers of theirs, therefore, we are caught in the middle. We often speak about reaching others for Christ but my outreach is not very satisfying. If I could at least get them to attend service that would be a source of consolation. They respect us highly and speak of our close family ties. But reaching them seems.... far fetched... If not futile.

Theresa: Your position is understandable. In my experience as a single parent, I have learned to disregard the indifferent attitudes of some people; then pursue the path I think is best for Patricia and myself. No, I do not consider this selfish. My involvement in the community especially with children and the disabled is extensive. Putting my faith in action is a living testimony rather than prodding others with words they choose to ignore. I still remember them in prayers.

Patricia: (Exciting tone) Yes! Mom and I have lots of fun together. She takes out plenty of time with me. I have lots of playmates, in the neighborhood our Sunday school Teacher is really great! I love singing in groups and sometime I sing alone.

(Solo)

Johnny Waste: (Well dressed with dangling jewelry) After sitting in this meeting, you have aroused my consciousness for the better things in life. Many of you probably can attest to the fact that my spendthrift habits are getting me down. Occasionally I think of changing but... (shrugging shoulders) what's the use? Money and prestige are driving forces. Once hooked, you are really trapped in the lime-light. Well, I am not ready to change but will contribute to your organization.

Mary Haste: Things are going very well with me. Life has been kind, exciting and inviting to me. Having one's own transportation does not seem slow at my age. New on the agenda is an apartment. Then, you will have another meeting place. Summer is near and we should increase our activities and fellowship. What about a fund raising project to support a foreign event, perhaps a missionary tour?

Stella: An excellent idea. Suppose you chair the planning committee for this event?

Mary Haste: Gladly! May I select Latrice as co-chairperson? We will get it together.

Stella: No problem. Our next meeting will be at the Beavers at which time you may submit a progress report. The Times' children are here with us. We would love to have Betty and Jimmy involved in the activities of the Gleaners. Let us hear from them.

Jimmy: Enjoyed being here. What I have heard sounds interesting but somewhat different from the usual trend of things Will be looking forward to meeting the group.

Betty: Count me in. As mom says, "Join the crowd, there is much to learn."

Mother Nature: Thank you for selecting our home and children to foster the cause for Christianity. May you run with patience the race that is set before you, looking unto Jesus the Author and Finisher of our faith for endurance.

Stella: We express warmest appreciation for the doors opened to us, for your joining in our efforts to strengthen the minds and hands of young people; thereby enabling their lives to be more creative and productive.

Mother Nature: Before you leave, I would like to make two distinct presentations. Both are very, very special. The first... my copilot, your lifetime friend, observer and molder of your physical being – the unconquerable, Mr. Father Time.

Father Time: (Dressed more obsolete than earlier) How delighted I am to be a part of your life--From the cradle to the grave it is the in-between that counts most; meaning the manner in which you function to obtain a richer, fuller life. Keep in mind it is a gift from God. Someone had so wisely said, "Time waste is past; thou can'st not it recall; time is, thou hast; employ the portion small; time future is not; and may never be; time present, is the only time for thee." (bows gently) Enjoy life! (bows again).

Mother Nature: The other special is the musical presentation a super treat, a heart warming inspiring gift from God, meet...The Choral Group hear ye them! (Choral Group: Sings appropriate selections.)

The End

Prepared especially for the Prospect District Congress Young People's Department. Requested by Dean Verdie Robinson.

RETURN OF THE WAYWARD SON
(Dramatic version based on story of the Prodigal Son)

Characters
Father: Well-dressed businessman
Younger Son: Tattered, torn clothes replaced later
Older Son, Servant, Soloist

Setting on Stage - 2 chairs, table, Bible, flowers and some books.

Father: (Walking floor, seemingly despondent:) Here it is, the beginning of a New Year and I am hurting as never before; haven't heard from Phillip, seems as if he could have gotten a message to us somehow. Dead or alive! I want to know. My spirit is broken and my heart is getting weaker as time passes. Perhaps I gave him too much. I bent over backward trying to please him. I can only blame myself. The only thing left for me to do is to give him up into the hands of the Lord.

(Remove Bible from table and read entire Psalms 42 aloud, slowly and reverently.)

Soloist: (Off stage) Singing
"God answers prayers in the morning
God answers prayers at noon,
God answers prayers in the evening
And keeps your heart in tune." (repeat)

Father: What a relief! I am not sure but something good is going to happen.

(Soloist continues to sing above song while the father relaxes - approximately three minutes).

Father: I believe God is able to do all things. Lord, increase my faith as I wait.

Soloist: "Coming Home"

Younger Son: (Comes down the aisle on verse two of above hymn, unkept, tattered clothing; hair unkept.)

Father (rushes out to greet his son): My son! My son! Where have you been? I have grieved day and night for your return (hugging him tightly and warmly).

Younger Son: (Interrupts father) Father, I have sinned against heaven and in thy sight. Please forgive me. I am not worthy to be called your son any longer. Give me a servant's position that will satisfy me; I have been reckless and insensitive to your love and kindness.

Father: (Calls servant who comes) Welcome home, my long lost child. Get the best of clothing for him. Put a ring on his hand and shoes on his feet. Kill the fatted calf, let us eat and be merry.

(Younger son and servant exit while "Love Lifted Me" is being sung. They return. Time out for change of raiment may be used also for a related poem recital.)

Older Son: (Hears all the rejoicing, becomes angry, rushes by and shows his displeasure) What's all this noise about, Father? I have been here all this time, obeyed your command, never gave you any trouble; yet, you never gave a feast for me nor appreciated what I have done. As soon as this son of yours returns, who wasted his life and your substances on women of the night, you have gone all out for him. I give up on you and him. Goodbye.

As Father and Younger Son cleave to each other, last verse and chorus of "Love Lifted Me" by congregation is sung.

DELIVERANCES
(Easter)

It is suggested that various instruments be used to "Tell the *Story of Jesus*" in resounding tones, yet maintain its sweetness and sacredness. Examples: Organ, piano, saxophone, flute, tambourine, harp, trombone, etc. They may be used harmoniously or individually following each Speaker's presentation.

<u>Participants</u>: Six speakers, instrumentalists, soloists or choral group. If desired, some portion of events may be dramatized.

First Speaker: Easter is a time of rejoicing because Christ brought new life, hope and direction to a fallen generation as He triumphed over sin, death, hell and destruction. The women were profoundly affected on that gloomy Lord's Day as they visited the empty tomb. However, upon meeting the risen Savior, their sorrows were turned to joy; fears to trust; questions to answers, doubt to belief; emptiness to fullness and darkness to light. After this encounter, they were well prepared to share the Good News of the Resurrection with the disciples.

Today, those of us who have sought the Lord Jesus Christ accepted His principles of righteousness through faith and know beyond the shadow of a doubt that He lives within us <u>must</u> rejoice as living witnesses. Because He lives we shall live also.

Musical Selection: **"Because He Lives"**

Second Speaker: Let us review some Bible deliverances followed by praises and adorations to our Lord, Savior and King. Luke 8:43-48 The woman with the issue of blood was healed. (Use own *memory* to summarize story.)

Musical Selection: "He Touched Me"

Third Speaker: In the fourth chapter of Saint John, Christ crossed over racial, sexual and religious barriers by communicating with the Samaritan woman. (Relate story in own words.)

Musical Selection: "Love Lifted Me"

Fourth Speaker: Luke 19:1-10, we find the transformation of Zacchaeus after seeing Jesus. (Relate event.)

Musical Selection: "When I see Jesus, Amen"

Fifth Speaker: John 11:39-44. The raising of Lazarus from the dead demonstrated power over life and death. (Share the story.)

Musical Selection: "He Arose" (Up from the Grave)

Sixth Speaker: Luke 24:13-49 is the account of Jesus appearing to His disciples and reassuring them of His resurrection. (Share the Account.)

Musical Selections: "Jesus Christ Is Risen Today, Alleluia!"- "All Hail the Power of Jesus' Name"

All speakers seated on platform during service. Each rises at designated time to participate. All stand and join in singing the last song before exiting.

GRATITUDE UNLIMITED
(Skit)

NARRATOR: This skit is to remind us that God has truly blessed us and does not expect us to sit idly by and be contented with our lot. We are admonished to share our blessings whether they be spiritual, material or intellectual. We ask that you let your mind reflect on St. Luke, Chapter 17:12-19, the cleansing of the ten lepers. Scripture tells us that ten were healed but only a Samaritan returned and gave thanks. Our aim is to create a scene based on this, designed to inspire and to motivate gratitude and humility.

(Choir sings **"Jesus Loves the Little Children."**)

Near the end of the song, five lepers enter dressed in ragged robes and sandals. One sits at the gate. Second limps on a cane. Third stands around looking at his hands. Fourth bows as if in prayer. Fifth weeps and extends a cup for financial support when he approaches the Master.

Master enters.

SOLO: "O Lord Have Mercy"

The lepers approach the Master, all requesting help. They stand far off.

NARRATOR: The Master raised his right hand, healed them and instructed them to show themselves to the priest. The miracle of healing took place as they traveled. Should not this have been a time of rejoicing and thanksgiving? All continued on their way thankless except one. Their attitudes were to accept whatever came their way and be more ready to receive than to **give**-even a simple thank you. What about your attitude? Are your children taught to be grateful?

Fifth leper returns, thanks the Master, bows down at His feet and worships Him.

NARRATOR: As we approach the Thanksgiving Holiday with its traditional family gathering and turkey dinners, may we be truly grateful and sincere not giving mere lip service. Someone has said, "To be thankful means to be thinkful." As we think on the blessings of God, our hearts should over-flow with thanksgiving, demonstrating love to God and love for our fellowmen. God help us to possess unlimited gratitude and to seek opportunities to share our blessings with the less fortunate.

    Select appropriate song for closing.

WE THREE KINGS OF ORIENT ARE
Enjoy the dramatic presentation and beauty of this familiar Christmas Hymn penned by John H. Hopkins.

Characters:

3 Men - kingly roles (possessing singing ability, if possible; otherwise pantomime and use a soloist). Oriental costumes appropriate.

Woman- medium height representing the Star, draped in white garment with glittering starry headgear carrying flashing light.

Portrayals of Joseph and Mary sitting on stage beside a cradle which contains a large open Bible.

Setting: semi-dark auditorium. Kaleidoscopic lighting would enhance the scenery. Table near cradle for gifts from kings.

Begin with the kings offstage singing the chorus as they follow the Star, slowly but reverently, traveling westward.

Upon reaching the stage, the Star will posture herself near the setting of Joseph and Mary.

CHORUS:
O star of wonder, star of night Star of royal beauty bright,
Westward leading, still proceeding, Guide us to thy perfect light.

> Upon reaching the center of the stage,
> they sing together verse one:

We three Kings of Orient are
Bearing gifts we traverse afar
Field and fountain,
moor and mountain,
Following yonder star.

Following this, Kings number two and three steps backward as King number one moves forward to sing verse two:

Born a King on Bethlehem plain
Gold I bring to crown Him again,
King forever, ceasing never
Over us all to reign.
        (Carries a gift wrapped in gold paper.)

Second King moves forward to sing verse three as the first King steps backward still holding his gift.)

Frankincense to offer have I,
Incense owns a Deity nigh;
Prayer and praising,

(King number two bows his head, followed by lifting of his hand; first one and then the other shifting his gift which should be wrapped in lavender colored paper. Continue singing.)

All men raising,
Worship Him,
God on high.

Third King moves forward to sing fourth verse. (Gift wrapped in reddish-brown paper.) Myrrh is mine, its' bitter perfume

Breathes a life of
gathering doom;
Sorrowing, sighing,
bleeding, dying,
Sealed in the stone-cold tomb.

(Assume a distressful attitude.)

Together, all sing the fifth verse:

Glorious now behold Him arise,
King and God and Sacrifice;
Alleluia, Alleluia!
Peals through the earth and skies.

Kings bow beside the cradle in worshipful attitude, after placing gifts on table reverently. The Star exits off stage right and kings exit left as they continue to sing fifth verse.

THE END

CHRISTMAS: DECORATIVE & SPIRITUAL
(To involve the entire Church School) Narrative

More than 1900 years ago, a little babe was born in Bethlehem of Judea, where His birth had been foretold by prophets hundreds of years prior to His coming. His name was to be called Wonderful, Counselor, the Mighty God, the Everlasting Father, the Prince of Peace. "Thou shalt call his name Jesus for He shall save his people from their sins." In spite of this, the people were not able to accept Him because of the mysteries surrounding his birth.

The Advent of Christ unto the world has not only changed the course of history, but has also changed the lives of many. Most of the world celebrates the birthday of Christ but few people invite Him to be a part of this celebration.

Historians and writers have documented various customs and symbols used throughout the world at this time of the year. Let us examine some of these.

(As this is being narrated a boy enters holding a small Christmas tree)

**All participants will march in, keeping pace as much as possible with the music. Remain on stage about two minutes holding articles, place same on a prepared table and retire to the choir stand.

PART 1

THE CHRISTMAS TREE: The Christmas tree has been used in America approximately one hundred years ago. Evergreens are the most popular, though cactus, pines, palms and other varieties are used in sections which do not have evergreens. It has been said that all trees in the forest blossomed and bore fruit on the night of Christ's birth.

Martin Luther is credited with decorating the first Christmas tree in Germany following a walk through the forest on Christmas Eve when the stars shining through the evergreen trees impressed him so much he attempted to show his family a sight like it so he cut down an evergreen and decorated it with lighted candles.

In China the Christmas tree is called the "Tree of lights." The evergreen tree symbolized the everlasting life of Christ.

THE HOLLY: (A girl marches in carrying a holly wreath.)

It is significant that the holly which grows in almost every country has come to be a symbol of Christmas decoration. The fact that it is a wreath represents the crown of thorns placed on the head of Jesus when He was crucified. The red berries represent the blood which flowed down over his face. The hard, almost imperishable leaves of holly are a symbol of everlasting life-something which does not die.

THE BELLS: (A girl marches in carrying Christmas bells.) Two thousand years before Christ was born, bells were used in the Orient for joyful, as well as sad, occasions. They are used to announce the hour of twelve on Christmas Eve in Spain. Chimes proclaim the entrance of Christmas in some places in America. Bells are symbols of joyful sublime tidings.

GREETING CARDS: (Girl marches in carrying large Christmas card)

Greeting cards were first published in England in 1844 by Mr. Joseph Cundall and thus originated one of the most widely used customs today.

SEALS: (Child marches in carrying Christmas seals.)

It was the idea of a postal clerk in the Post Office in Copenhagen, Denmark, to issue a stamp for letters of Christmas time, the proceeds to be used for some worthy cause. In the United States, Christmas seals are used to fight tuberculosis.

SELECTION: **Children's Choir**

MISTLETOE: (Child enters carrying mistletoe)

When used in connection with the Christmas festivities in the United States, it causes much merriment and to those who choose to give it meaning, the white berries represent the purity and the leaves the everlasting life of the Babe.

CANDLES: (Child enters carrying candles)

Tri-colored candles are sometimes used in honor of the Trinity, one lighted on Christmas Eve, another on Christmas Day and the third on New Year's Eve.

OIL LAMPS: (Child marches in carrying oil lamp)

On Christmas Eve, tiny oil lamps are lighted in the homes in Spain and other countries. They are also used in some place to light the churches for the Christmas Eve services.

STOCKINGS: (Child marches in with stockings)

Stockings are used by children in the United States of America to receive the gifts of Santa Claus. They are also used in some European countries.

SANTA CLAUS: (Santa Claus strolls down the aisle)

Santa Claus is said to descend from Saint Nicholas of European origin, always kind, thoughtful, doing good deeds to rich and poor alike. The fat, jolly, red robed figure represents the spirit of giving at Christmas time.

GIFTS: (Two children march in carrying gift-wrapped parcels.)

Christ is the "Gift of God" to the world. The Wise Men came bearing gifts to the Babe.

Through the ages, people have given gifts to those they love and to others less fortunate in honor of the Wise Men, the first gift bearers in the Christian era.

MINCE PIES: (Child enters carrying pie)

Mince pies were used in ancient times to represent the manger. The contents were supposed to commemorate, in their mixture, the spices which the Wise Men gave to the Christ Child.

SELECTION: "Hark the Herald Angles Sing"

OFFERING

CHRISTMAS: DECORATIVE & SPIRITUAL
PART II

POINSETTIA: (Child enters carrying Poinsettia)

Dr. Joel Poinset, a minister to Mexico, is credited with bringing this wild plant to the United States and using it as a Christmas flower. The shape of the red flower is like many pointed stars which give it real meaning as a Christmas plant.

ROSE: (Child enters carrying a rose)

The" Christmas Rose" is often used to decorate homes and trees in Central Europe. To some the use of the " fairest flower that blows" is a fitting symbol for the "fairest babe ever born," Christ is called the Rose of Sharon.

MUSIC:" It Came Upon a Midnight Clear."

(Stage has been set with a manger. Mary and Joseph march in and lean fervently over the manger.)

Angel marches in.

SHEPHERDS: "And there were shepherds abiding in the field, keeping watch over their flock by night. And lo, the Angel of the Lord came upon them and the glory of the Lord shone round about them." Luke 2:8-9.

And they came with haste and found Mary and Joseph and the Babe lying in a manger. Luke 2:16.

STAR: (A tall person draped in a white sheet with a large silver star pasted on as a headgear, marches in followed by the Wise Men. Upon reaching the stage, the Star stands still and the Wise Men sing " We Three Kings." Wise Men will carry gifts.

CROSS: (Child enters carrying a cross.)

The cross is more appropriately used as the Easter symbol, but in some countries, a cross is placed in front of the homes to keep away evil. Lighted crosses indicate the Living Christ as the Light of the World. He is light and in Him there is no darkness. If you would be wise today, seek Christ as did the Wise Men, let the light of His love shine through you and dedicate yourself to His service and to humanity, thereby making the world a better place to live in.

SELECTION "Joy to the World"

REMARKS BENEDICTION

RESOURCES

The Holy Bible-King James Version

Life Application Bible-Tyndale House Publishers, Inc.

The Living Bible (Paraphrased) Tyndale House Publishers, Copyright 1971

Nelson Illustrated Bible Dictionary-Thomas Nelson Publishers 1978

The Thompson Chain Reference Bible-Frank Charles Thompson, D.D. Ed.D. B.B. Kirkbride Bible CC., Inc. Copyright 1982

New Bible Dictionary-J.D. Douglas

Webster New Collegiate Dictionary-Merriam-Webster Everyone In The Bible-William P. Barker 1966 Edition *Your Bible-R.* Laird, Ph.D. Revised Edition 1976

*God's Word B.C.-*John W. Wade

Winning and Keeping Teens In The Church- Melvin E. Banks, Urban Ministries, Inc. 1970 Edition, Detroit Public Library

1800 Quotable Quotes-E. C. McKenzie Baker Book House. Grand Rapids, Michigan 1970 Edition

IN LOVING MEMORIES OF
MR. GRANDERSON BROWN
1913 – 2011

In loving memories of my God sent, wonderful, devoted, Christ-centered husband, Granderson Brown. Grant, as frequently as having been called, passed this life on the twentieth day of August in the year of our Lord 2011.

The joy of the Lord was upon us for having permitted us to enjoy more than fifty years together in marital bliss. He died at the age of ninety-eight, leaving me at eighty-nine years. Lonesome? Yes! But not alone. God knows what is best. In my heart and mind <u>Grant still lives</u>.

To God Be the Glory for all of the great things He has done in our lives.

Thank You Lord! To God Be The Glory!

Your Loving Wife, Martha! Martha!
Family and Friends

MEMORIAL MEDITATION
("Abide With Me" – Music Softly)

*"He that dwelleth in the secret place of the Most High
shall abide under the shadow of the Almighty. I will say of the Lord.
He is my refuge and my fortress: my God; in him will I trust."*

Psalm 91:1-2

We know by abiding in Him, we shall reign with Him forever and ever. Life on this planet is indeed a journey not a long one but a short one, filled with diversities from the cradle to the grave. Each encounters a little sunshine here, a bit of rain there; moments of laughter, hours of sorrows; few friends, numerous opponents; some frustration and scarcely any relaxation. In the midst of this if one keeps faith and hope alive, there is abundant joy waiting at the end of the day.

Today we thank God for the lives of those who abide in Him. They are not present but their labor, influence, contributions and associations have left indelible imprints here, in the community, district and state organizations.

We pause to pay tribute to our beloved friends whose memories are sweet, precious and enduring.

(Close with short prayer.)

www.ingramcontent.com/pod-product-compliance
Lightning Source LLC
Chambersburg PA
CBHW052028070526
44584CB00016B/1945